# Praise of "Peace Smarts" Team

*"Thank you for the work you are doing for our children."*
President Clinton

*"I've watched you...You are doing a great job."*
Oprah Winfrey

*"I want to thank you again for all you have shared, your stories, your support, and dedication to building a world of kindness and acceptance."*
Co-founder's Cynthia Germanotta and Lady Gaga
Born This Way Foundation

*"Merrie Lynn Ross, it is an honor to present you with the 'Humanitarian Peace Award' for your dedication, visionary insight, and the hope you give parents and children to create a world of unity and peace."*
Four Worlds International

*"Peace Smarts saved my life. I was 13- years old, using drugs, and hanging out with the wrong people. Thank you for mentoring me, and helping to turn my life around."* Jeremy K. 11th grade.

*"Girl Scouts have benefited across the nation, learning ethical tools in the Peace Smarts curriculum. Merrie Lynn, unanimous kudos for your inspirational energy to help our families grow strong."* Sheila Lewis, Girl Scouts of America.
*"Merrie Lynn your anti-bully project is needed in our schools and community. Keep the plan rolling forward."* Sheriff Lee Baca, Los Angeles County.

# PEACE SMARTS™

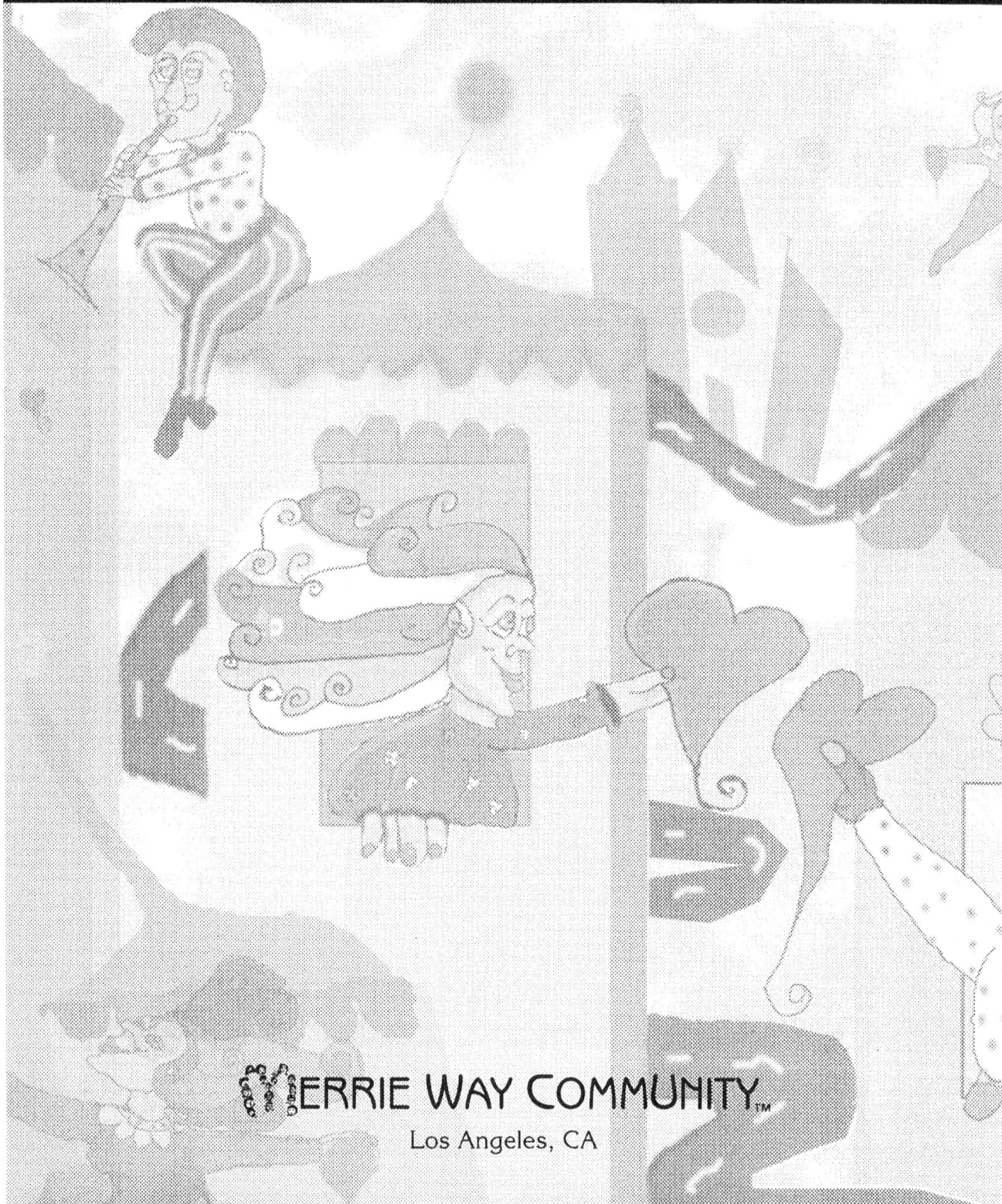

**MERRIE WAY COMMUNITY™**
Los Angeles, CA

## Merrie Lynn Ross
## Gloria DeGaetano, M. Ed.

# PEACE SMARTS

# MERRIE LYNN ROSS

# GLORIA DEGAETANO M.Ed

Sketch – Byron Fox

# In loving memory of my beloved son, Byron Fox

You shine on as a Loving Peacemaker. As our National Spokesperson, you served with enthusiasm, joy and dedication. A magical inspiration...you touched many hearts in your glorious 22 years.

Your enlivened spirit radiates your wish for us to...

## "BE Real, Laugh & Love"

# ACKNOWLEDGMENTS

Heartfelt Gratitude to the amazing global participants in "Peace Smarts." To the students, parents, teachers, administrators for contributing their ingenuity and commitment to create a culture of peace. To MerrieWay Community for offering the stellar "Peace Smarts" program and exercises included here.

We thank our sponsors: Microsoft, Ellis Foundation, Lorsch Family Foundation, Lear Foundation, Roger Dauer, Sheriff Baca, Los Angeles, New York, Texas, and Washington School Districts, Chicago Police Veterans, Darby Mcfarland, Madeline Guzzman, Write Brothers. Philanthropists, community activists, and other contributors, too many to mention, you know who you are.

Your commitment, resourcefulness, and courage sets an example, raises the bar, bringing together the heart and soul of our society... to live the highest ethical standards for the benefit of all.

Bravo to our "Peace Smarts" Youth Anchor team, our masterful mentors, volunteers, and facilitators, who are our Heart Song, spreading unity's light, passing the torch of peace, One by One.

# Table of Contents

# PEACE SMARTS
## A Call to Action

"As human beings, our greatness lies not so much in being able to remake the world
...as in being able to remake ourselves."

—————————————— Gandhi ——————————————

**Peace Smarts,** created by **Merrie Way Community,** supports, encourages, and guides youth/teens toward a peaceful lifestyle. This comprehensive program teaches and **inspires a "peace culture," in both the inner world (of self) and the outer world (of connection to others). Peace Smarts** engages youth in collaborative, grassroots efforts, and in so doing, helps to create safe communities.

**Peace Smarts** is youth-centered and youth-focused. It is specifically designed for those working with youth: teachers, counselors, youth advocates, police officers, social workers, and community volunteers. **Peace Smarts** facilitators working with youth, ages 10-18, can readily transmit innovative ideas, teach practical skills, and cultivate community-based decision-making regarding the violence embedded in our culture.

The ideas and techniques in this manual teach core social skills, character traits, and problem-solving abilities needed to counteract and prevent violence. Cultivating an intuitive understanding by youth that non-violence is the higher road and the way to go, elicits an upliftment of attitude and response. The core of the program's effectiveness is a well-defined sequence of **"Morphing Violence Into Peace,"** children and teens have numerous opportunities to:

* re-construct their beliefs and attitudes to embrace larger possibilities of non-violence in their daily lives;

* re-create their actions to reflect peace-filled lives; and

* re-invent methods of peace-making and collaborations with authorities such as the police, to know first-hand the joy of a compassionate world.

Basically, **Peace Smarts** is a transformational problem-solving approach which brings hope and teaches creative solution finding.

In Peace Smarts we superimpose one image, thought, concept, over another to improve; to transform; to find positive solutions to human issues and concerns; to evolve and create a vision of hope and inspiration for humanity.

Practicing **Peace Smarts** results in a "meta**morph**asis" from violence to peace, in thoughts, attitudes, values, and actions.

**6**

# PROGRAM GOALS

## Specifically Peace Smarts:

* Provides **NEW** **innovative strategies** for community-based violence prevention programs

* Provides a concrete method of **solution-finding**, a transformational process which youth can learn to apply to any given situation for the rest of their lives.

* Provides ways to instruct youth in **conflict resolution**, peace-smart **problem-solving** approaches and core **interpersonal skills** for living in peace.

* Promotes the cause of peace by showing youth how to practice **nonviolence and tolerance** in their lives, in all the different environments they encounter daily.

* Increases the positive awareness that police are friends whom youth can turn to for protection and guidance by **encouraging attitudes of respect** and reverence for adults in authority.

* Brings recognition to police organizations, crime and gang prevention programs, and other community **organizations devoted to addressing violence**, guiding youth to know that these people are there to serve, protect, and empower them.

* Provides **projects for youth collaboration** with police and community programs by showing ways youth can form teams with adults to "morph" violence into peace.

* Provides principles, ethical standards, and action projects to **positively engage youth**

* Promotes tolerance, celebration of diversity, social justice, cooperative learning, and community service by **helping youth to effect change on grassroots levels**, helping youth feel needed for the common good.

* Demonstrates the **value of community involvement** and living a service-oriented life.

# YOUTH VIOLENCE: THE PROBLEM

We have heard it often enough, "our youth are at risk", but sometimes the statistics can delineate the complexities of the problem. Consider these statistics from *The Real War on Crime: The Report of the National Criminal Justice Commission*, for instance:

* The risk of being a victim of a serious crime is nearly four times higher for a person 16-19 years old than it is for a person aged 35-49.

* Researchers have found that increases in gang killings in Chicago resulted almost exclusively from high-tech firearms available to young people, not more incidents of shooting.

* Between 1986 and 1992, the number of children in the United States killed by firearms jumped 144%, compared to a 30% increase for adults.

* The justice system is spending more than $3.2 billion each year to keep children in custody.

> If we were fighting an outside enemy that was killing our children at a rate of more than five thousand a year we would spare no expense in mounting the effort to subdue that enemy. What happens when that enemy is us?...Do we still have the will to invest the time and resources in saving their lives? The answer must be yes, because the impact and fear of violence has overrun the boundaries of our ghettos and has both its hands firmly around the neck of the whole country.
>
> _____ **Geoffrey Canada, *FistStickKnifeGun*** _____

## 8

# RISK FACTORS

## Previous Experience of Violence

In its summary report, *Violence and Youth: Psychology's Response, the Commission on Violence and Youth* of the American Psychological Association cited research indicating that the strongest predictor of a child's involvement with violence is a history of previous violence. Noted psychologist Ronald Slaby found that children involved in violence in the preteen or teenage years (as victims or perpetrators) are highly likely to have been victims of child abuse or bullying, or have witnessed violence in the home earlier in their lives.

## Social and Cultural Factors:

* poverty
* domestic violence
* prejudice and racism
* access to firearms
* drugs and alcohol
* gang behaviors lead to delinquency, teen homicides and assaults
* Also, exposure to high levels of media violence has a cumulative effect, increasing aggression and meanness, callousness, and apathy.

## Daily Domains:

In the book, *Safe by Design: Planning for Peaceful Communities*, distinguished researchers David Hawkins and Richard Catalano explain that risk factors tend to be reinforced across the child's social spheres, including family, school, peer groups, and the community:

* *Individual risk factors*: failure to bond to positive institutions or organizations, having inadequately developed social skills, or having friends who engage in violent behavior.

* *Family risk factors*: Families in which conflict is common and parents who fail to monitor or convey clear expectations for the children's behavior are more likely to produce children who will be involved in violence.

* *School risk factors*: Risk is greatest:

    **when** the community lacks crime prevention programs

    **when** high rates of vandalism and truancy go unchecked

    **when** there's little or no parental involvement and no positive mentors and role models

    **when** public areas are not patrolled

    **when** the community doesn't mobilize to stop crime, harassment, and youth infractions of the law

    **when** the community and the peace officers do not work together

# RISK FACTORS

Exposure to these risk factors can exert a damaging influence upon a child's future, but this exposure can be countered by preventive programs working to enhance protective factors. In 1993, the Office of Juvenile Justice and Delinquency Prevention (OJJDP), put forth a document entitled *Comprehensive Strategy for Serious Violent and Chronic Juvenile Offender*. The prevention approach advocated focused on minimizing risk factors that pushed youth toward delinquency and encouraged strengthening those institutions that had the most influence over young people—families, schools, peer groups, religious affiliations, and neighborhood and community programs.

Nothing can replace the importance and long-lasting positive effects of responsible adults guiding and leading our youth. Community violence prevention programs are critical to engaging families, schools, and agencies in this endeavor.

> We all know that, if we love our kids, money <u>must</u> be spent on inoculations, immunizations, food sanitation, and disease prevention. We understand that money spent on preventive medicine saves untold millions of dollars and prevents tragic, needless suffering. In the same way, community violence prevention programs are every bit as important as other forms of preventive medicine, and money spent in this vital area has enormous potential for saving untold thousands of dollars and preventing some of our society's tragic and destructive suffering.
> **Lt. Col. David Grossman, Professor of Military Science at Arkansas State University and author**
> **of *On Killing: The Psychological Cost of Learning to Kill in War and Society***

## 10

# PEACE SMARTS: THE SOLUTION

**Peace Smarts** systematically addresses the three protective factors determined by the recent research on resiliency. Studies show that children and teens are less likely to be involved in violence when families, schools, and communities:

* offer caring and support

* convey high expectations

* provide opportunities for youth to participate in violence prevention programs

In a comprehensive report, the Carnegie Council on Adolescent Development found that the most successful programs met the needs of youth. These five basic needs are listed below with ways the **Peace Smarts Program** addresses them.

| **Needs of Adolescents** | **Opportunities Through Peace Smarts** |
| --- | --- |
| Opportunities to bond in stable relationships with adults. | Mentoring and coaching relationships; collaborative **Peace Projects**. |
| Comfortable, friendly environment for relaxation and stimulation with friends. | Team building; peer interactions; relaxation techniques; stress management; discussion sessions to put teens at ease. |
| The chance to develop life-skills. | Learning the **PEACE Smart Process**; a solution-finding process which youth can apply to any problem throughout their lives; **Peace Tools** which teach essential life-skills in conflict resolution, stress reduction, metacognitive self-talk, negotiation, assertivenesstraining, and preventive skills for steering clear of a violent lifestyle. |
| The chance to contribute to their community. | A community-based program emphasizing youth involvement. |
| Opportunities to feel competent and skillful. | Encouragement for youth to think critically and creatively and to take action |

# PEACE SMARTS: THE SOLUTION

**Peace Smarts** facilitators and parents must create a safe environment for children and teens to communicate freely their needs, issues, and what's troubling them.

**Peace Smarts** can benefit *all* youths, from the "average" to "at-risk" to the hardened gang member, giving all important peace-smart skills. Although the largest amount of violence and the most serious violent acts are committed by a small number of youths, all youths to some degree suffer the effects of our violent culture. Having a friend whose parents are involved in domestic violence; trying to learn in a classroom whose environment is one of fear and hate; attending a party where someone brings a gun—all these common experiences necessitate peace-smart attitudes and behaviors on the part of all of today's youth.

The **Peace Smarts Program** can assist schools, police, and other agencies in creating community efforts, engaging youth in the process, too. It has been said, "Great changes come in a time of rising expectations."[1] Let us now look at ways to change our communities by raising the expectations of our youth and guiding them to meet the challenges of these new expectations. Now, let us look at how the

# Peace Smarts Program

# can help make those

# "great changes…"

---

1   Ellen Goodman, "Moving Beyond the Mantra for Personal Responsibility,"

in *The Seattle Times*, November 21, 1997, p. B6

# Chapter 1

# The
# PEACE SMARTS
## Model

Peace Smarts uses three basic approaches to empower youth:

1. **The PEACE Smart Process**, a specific problem-solving sequence that teaches children and teens to create solutions concerning violence.

2. **Peace Tools**, or **peace-smart activities**, which help youths learn specific strategies for conflict resolution and for adopting peaceful attitudes and behaviors.

3. **Peace Projects** for youths to do, with the help of adults and in collaboration with the community.

## I. The PEACE Smart Process

**Peace Smarts** trains youth to learn practical ways to manifest peace—in their lives and in their communities— through an adaptation of the **Morphing Process**. (See *Morphing of America: Vol. 1 Morphing Across Curriculum*, Merrie Way Community, 1997.) Used by teachers and youth advocates, this process helps teens constructively address important societal issues by teaching a transformational problem solving/solution-finding process. The **PEACE Smart Process**, uniquely intended as a tool to help youth "morph violence into peace," can be used alone or in conjunction with **Morphing of America**.

This **PEACE Smart Process** involves five basic steps. It is intended that all five steps become routine as you teach and train youth in the **Process. Notice that the explanation for each step is written directly to the student. Please duplicate the steps, read and discuss them with the youths as they learn and experience this powerful process.**

# MORPH VIOLENCE INTO PEACE!

## Step 1: Prepare/Picture Possibilities

Prepare to set a course of action by choosing the specific issue that will be morphed. The issue can be whatever matters most at the time. The issue could be personal or more community-based. For instance, personal choices such as changing attitudes about violence, implementing habits of quieting the mind or learning to respond carefully rather than react hastily, are all relevant personal issues. Community concerns or general issues such as: dealing more effectively with bullies at your school or helping police officers implement a gang awareness program in the neighborhood are examples of what you could choose.

### Use the following steps to select your issue:

*   **Brainstorm** alone or with a group. **List all the possibilities**. The sky is the limit here. Picture possibilities that may seem far out at the time. It's OK to think far-fetched because that's a great way to stumble across a great idea. Give your imagination full range and have fun imaging what needs to be fixed. Don't worry about HOW in this step—just think about **WHAT**.

    Once you have a list of **WHAT's,** narrow your list down to **the most important one.** Some ways to do that could include:

*   **Prioritize the needs**. What would be the issues you would want to change given ideal circumstance?

*   **Talk with someone you trust.** Discuss how you are personally affected by violence and what you can do to make your environment more peaceful.

*   **Pick five issues** which are important to you. Write each on a slip of paper. Fold each paper. But them in a bowl or a hat and… **CHOOSE!**

### When you are finished with Step 1:

*   you have identified an issue about violence that you want to change.

# YOU HAVE A "WHAT!"

## Step 2: **Encourage Yourself and Others**

Sometime issues of violence can seem overwhelming. Before you go any further, it's important to encourage yourself and those you will be working with. Your feelings about what you chose in Step 1 are very important to acknowledge and discuss. In this step, with your adult facilitator:

* Talk about what seems scary or difficult about the violent issue you have chosen. Is there something about it that makes you feel uneasy? Anything that causes you to doubt yourself or your abilities to make positive changes?

* Get all your negative feelings out on the table so that you know what feelings you have that might be standing in your way from doing your best. Share and discuss these with the others you will be working with.

* Now, for the fun part. Take each negative feeling or discouraging idea and turn it around into something encouraging and hopeful. Come up with even more ideas for your project that will help you feel more encouraged. For instance, say you and your group have chosen to address the issue of violent toys. You are feeling discouraged because you don't know how to stop violent toys from influencing young children. The issue looks too big to tackle. After you have discussed your feelings about this, you and your group select the following ideas that can help you feel more encouraged:

* randomly interview parents about what they think about violent toys

* visit local toys stores and request that they stock only non-violent toys and games

### When you are finished with Step 2:

* you have identified and discussed any discouraging feelings or ideas, and

* you have faith in your ability to make a difference

# YOU HAVE ENCOURAGEMENT!

## Step 3: **Accept What Can and Can't Be Changed**

It's very human to want to do the very best in what we undertake. Issues of violence are complex, though, and often, we must address them one baby step at a time. We can't change everything, but we can change something. In this step you will identify what is realistic for you to change and what can't be changed—what you have to let go of so you can maintain your own inner peace and harmony about your actions. It doesn't help you or anyone else, for that matter, to hang onto those things which are out of your control. So, remember, whatever the course of action you take toward peace, you have done a noble project and saw something that needed to be done and did it. Congratulate yourself and let go of anything that is out of your control. Maintain the attitude that you are doing all you can do in the situation, and that, certainly, is enough.

### With your adult facilitator:

* Make a list of what is under your control to change in this project and another list of possible worries for which you are not responsible.

* Share and discuss these with others you may be working with.

* Then sitting in a circle with the others, state what you are letting go of, what you are accepting that, for now, you are not trying to change.

### When you are finished with Step 3:

* you have identified what you can and can't change during your peace project, and

* you are maintaining an attitude of confidence and calm assurance about the changes you are going to make.

# YOU HAVE FAITH!

**16**

## Step 4: **Choose an Action**

You might know before this time what you want to do. The threads of ideas are being formed in the first three steps as you consider your feelings and attitudes about the issue you have chosen. In this step you will refine what you want to do. In our example, the issue was violent toys and doing something meaningful about them. In thinking about what could be encouraging to do, the ideas to talk with parents and visit local toy stores came up in Step 2. In this step, the basic course of action was developed to collect violent toys and take them to the local recycling center, in addition to interviewing some parents and visiting local toy stores.

As you discuss with the adult facilitator possible peace project ideas, you may want to consider the following before you take action:

* Who will have specific responsibilities?

* What are these responsibilities?

* What is the time frame for your project?

Please refer to the **Peace Projects** at the end of each chapter for possible ideas about what to do.

### At the end of Step 4:

* You have chosen an action and taken it!

# YOU HAVE DONE SOMETHING!

# MORPH VIOLENCE INTO PEACE!

## Step 5: Evaluate the Results

This doesn't have to be a very complicated step, but it would be good to know what influence your project had on the people involved. Getting back to our example of the violent toy collection, the ways to evaluate it were decided as:

* Immediately after the collection, discuss with the teen group and the adult facilitator how they thought things went and how they feel about what happened.

* One month after the collection revisit some parents and talk with them about the drive and how having given up the violent toys has affected them and their children.

In Step 5, you discuss with others how they experienced the project, what they got out of it, and possibly what they may want to do next as a result of participating in this project.

### At the end of Step 5:

* You have gotten feedback from others about how your peace project has influenced them.

# YOU KNOW HOW IT WORKED!

## 18

# MORPH VIOLENCE INTO PEACE!

## Harmony in Thoughts, Feelings and Actions

The **PEACE Smart Process** supports the most recent research on brain-mind-body connections which acknowledges that change in behaviors are more apt to be long-term when human thoughts, feelings, and actions are all in harmony.[1] When moving through the **PEACE Smart Process**, youth experience opportunities to frame their thoughts in Steps 1, 3, 4, and 5. In Step 2, they identify, share, and discuss feelings. In Steps 4 and 5, they take practical actions.

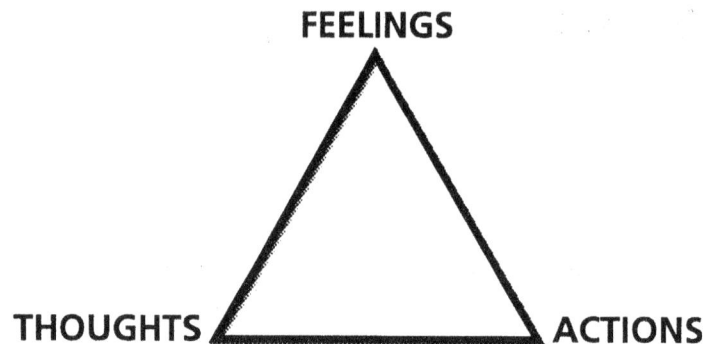

**FEELINGS**

**THOUGHTS** **ACTIONS**

Transformational, long-term results are more likely to occur when thoughts, feelings, and actions are all in harmony.

## II. Peace Tools

The second approach used to involve youth is through the **Peace Tools**. These are activities designed as reproducible pages for individual or group work. They can be used to get teens thinking about an issue and to teach them practical, needed information. They are intended to be used under the direction of an adult facilitator. They provide an avenue for youth to:

* gather additional information

* practice team-building skills

* learn group interaction skills

Peace Tools stand alone as mini-lessons, or can be used at various times throughout the five-step **PEACE Smart Process**. Think of **Peace Tools** as "coaches on paper" to help children and teens more thoroughly examine the issues.

---

1 Donald Curtis, *Your Thoughts Can Change Your Life*, Warner Nooks, 1996, p.103

## THE PEACE SMART PROCESS

# *P*repare/Picture Possibilities

# *E*ncourage Yourself and Others

# *A*ccept What Can and Can't be Changed

# *C*hoose a Course of Action

# *E*valuate the Results

## III. PEACE Projects

These are projects youths can do at home, with friends, in their schools, or communities as ways to promote peace. They are found at the back of chapters 2-7. Most projects involve collaboration between the youth and other organizations such as with police or other community resources.

**This manual addresses six specific topics in Chapters 2-7:**

**Chapter 2:** Becoming Peace-Smart—focus on personal choices, decision-making

**Chapter 3:** Family Peace Smarts—peace tools for parents as well as teens

**Chapter 4:** Peace Smarts at School—ways to empower youth at school

**Chapter 5:** Keeping Relationships Peace-Smart—information and skills needed

for safe relationships

**Chapter 6:** Peace-Smart Neighborhoods—ways to involve youth in

community-based violence prevention programs

**Chapter 7:** Practicing Peace Smarts—strategies and skills for youth to practice

during daily routine

Each chapter contains **Peace Tools, Peace Projects (both described above) and**:

## Discussion Questions

These questions can be used in different settings such as: in the classroom; at youth centers, during church-affiliated programs, or in teen advocacy groups to discuss with young people their roles and responsibilities for being peace-smart. Use these questions to help children and teens:

*   explore both the value of learning to communicate and cooperate as a group, examine their personal roles as individuals in creating peace-smart environments, and

*   express feelings and ideas about violence prevention

Provocative questions help spur youth discussion on a variety of topics related to the chapter's central theme. Real life questions rarely can be answered with a "yes" or a "no." These questions demand thinking and offer mental challenges. The facilitator should strive to bring out ideas and nurture high level thinking and creative answers. Youth need time and space to "be heard." These discussion sessions can serve to give youths a safe place to express themselves. You will note that there are many open-ended questions. These invite students to confront tough issues and controversial subjects. Occasionally, students are also invited to share a personal experience. The facilitator should never push these invitations. But sharing personal experiences with violence can, of course, be powerful entries into meaningful solutions. These 25 discussion questions appear after the short introduction page. You can use them in a variety of meaningful ways. But we recommend that you use them to introduce the chapter about to be studied and to gather information about where the children or teens stand on this topic.

## Options for Using This Manual

The design of this manual gives much flexibility to the adult facilitator. Some options include:

**1.** Use the **PEACE Smart Process** to guide youth to implement a **Peace Project** on a given topic. This five-step creative solution-finding approach gives a basic structure children or teens can use repeatedly to transform issues of violence into peace.

**2.** Use the **Discussion Questions** and **Peace Tools** to teach peaceful character traits and personal peace-smart strategies.

**3.** Use the **Peace Projects** in any given chapter to motivate children and teens to get involved in their community.

**4.** Use **Peace Tools** along with the **PEACE Smart Process** to teach a detailed problem-solving sequence related to a particular issue of violence.

**5.** Choose a need in your school, organization, or community. Pick **Peace Tools** and **Peace Projects** that can involve children or teens in addressing that need.

# Chapter 2

# BECOMING PEACE-SMART

Since 1993 many existing programs have shifted emphasis to issues of youth violence and many new programs have also been created to address the problem. What appears to work most effectively is a combination of:

* immediate intervention when delinquency occurs and

* a holistic approach in supporting youth.

If a child starts missing school or shoplifts a candy bar—these are red flags which call for immediate intervention. Then, along with the intervention must come the on-going support. As Sgt. Kumazec of the Cleveland Police Gang Unit points out, "We must support the kids from a lot of angles, that's why we use a multi-prong approach here in Cleveland, including establishing a curfew, instituting programs for children who witness violence, and having our police officers work closely with the schools."[1]

**The Peace Smarts Model** advocates and champions immediate intervention and a systems-approach to support our youth in the prevention and intervention of a violent life-style. Buoyed by academic research on adolescent development, **Peace Smarts** recognizes that any long-lasting change in youth behavior **must begin with the youth themselves**—their perceptions, belief systems, self-knowledge, and self-respect. In this chapter, we address these issues and provide Peace Tools for youth to:

* Define own concepts of peace and a non-violent approach to life. (Peace Tools # 1-5)

* Increase awareness of violence prevention; learn and practice communication and conflict resolution skills. (Peace Tools # 6-13)

* Learn specific strategies for managing anger and stress. (Peace Tools # 14-16 )

* Find hope, strength, and encouragement within oneself to live a non-violent lifestyle. (Peace Tools # 17-19)

---

1   Telephone Interview, September 23, 1997

# For Discussion

1. Do we as a society have what it takes to live non-violently? Why or why not?

2. What does it take personally to opt for peace instead of violence?

3. What are the roots of violence? How do these roots grow in individuals?

4. What does peace look like? What does violence look like?

5. What does being peace-smart mean to you?

6. Describe a person you know who has "inner peace"? How can you tell by his or her actions that this person is at peace?

7. Are you at peace inside yourself? How can you tell? If not, how can you get there?

8. Is violence or peace more interesting? Why? How do you define "interesting" in this instance?

9. Why is being peaceful more mature than being violent? Explain.

10. What do you do in your life to promote non-violence?

11. What would you recommend as the most important things people can do to promote peace and cooperation?

12. Pretend you are in a "think tank of the future," what ideas do you have for helping people and societies live in peace?

13. How have you personally been affected by violence? What did you do as a result?

14. How do a person's thoughts contribute to making a violent society?

15. If you had to give advice to a young child about not taking up a violent lifestyle, what would you say to him or her?

16. If you gave advice to a peer about not taking up a violent lifestyle, what would you say to him or her?

17. Who are the supportive people in your life who can help you become more peace-smart?

18. What are the personal reasons for becoming peace-smart?

19. What are the societal reasons for becoming peace-smart?

20. What does being peace-smart give to you? to others? to society in general?

21. What prohibits some from becoming peace-smart?

22. What is the one thing you can do today to become more peace-smart?

23. Describe society five years from now. What have you done to help make a more peaceful world?

24. What does it mean: "to develop a social conscience?" How would you do that?

25. Describe a typical day of a person who is peace-smart.

**Peace Tool # 1**

# PEACE IN YOUR LIFE

**Directions:** In the space below each question, jot down some of your ideas and then discuss them with a partner or in a small group.

\*      How are your ideas about peace the same? different?

\*      What have you learned from one another?

**1.** Give a few words which would describe a person "living a peaceful lifestyle."

_____

_____

_____

**2.** Think about a person (real or imagined) who is peaceful, then below describe the following about that person:

**thoughts:**
_____

**feelings:**
_____

**actions:**
_____

**3.** What do you admire the most about the person you described above? Why?

_____

_____

_____

**4.** List three things which hinder you from being as peaceful as you want to be.

_____

_____

_____

**5.** What do you need to learn about yourself to become more peaceful?

_____

_____

_____

**6.** How can you start today, right now, learning what is needed?

_____

_____

_____

**Peace Tool # 2**

# THE ROOTS OF VIOLENCE

## Directions: The roots or causes of violence can be many.

Below are given some of the roots of violence in our society. What can these roots grow?

* On the branches of the tree, list the possible violent consequences, or growths, from these negative roots.

* For instance, two possible results could be more murders and increase in gangs. Write on the branches *anything* that you think can grow from such roots.

* When you are finished discuss your ideas with others and then do the **Quiet Activity** below.

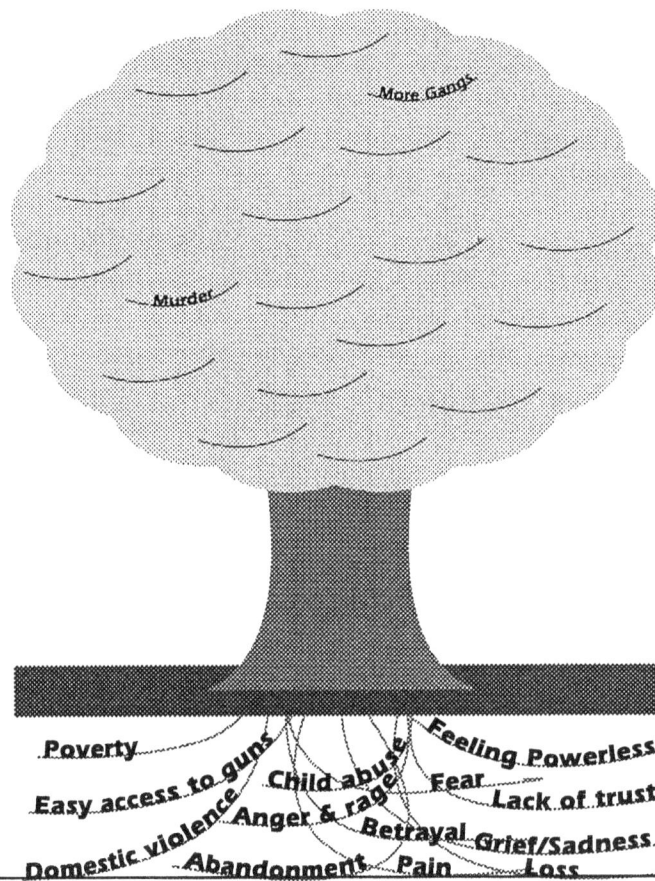

More Gangs

Murder

Poverty

Easy access to guns   Child abuse   Fear

Feeling Powerless

Lack of trust

Domestic violence   Anger & rage

Betrayal   Grief/Sadness

Abandonment   Pain   Loss

**Quiet Activity:** Close your eyes and go within. Take a few deep breaths and imagine... you and your friends are pulling out these negative roots one by one. Carefully pick up the roots and take them to the bonfire waiting close by to burn them. Make sure you get all the little pieces. If a root breaks off, as they often do, see yourself with a spade digging out the root to its very core. Get a friend to help you. Now, make sure all the roots are gone and turn over the soil until you are satisfied that it is all clean, free of all the negative roots. Now you are ready to sow important seeds. Open your eyes slowly and stretch... Go on to Peace Tool #3.

## Peace Tool # 3

# SOW THE SEEDS OF NON-VIOLENCE

**Directions:** Below you are "seeds" that will grow into many expressions of non-violence.

*   On the "blank seeds" write what you think should be planted for more peace to grow in your life and in society.

*   Then on top of the soil, (in the space below) draw new growth such as trees, plants, or flowers, and tell what each represents. For instance, some seeds could be positive thoughts and new flowers could be "patience with other people," "kindness to my little brother," and "more friendly people in the world."

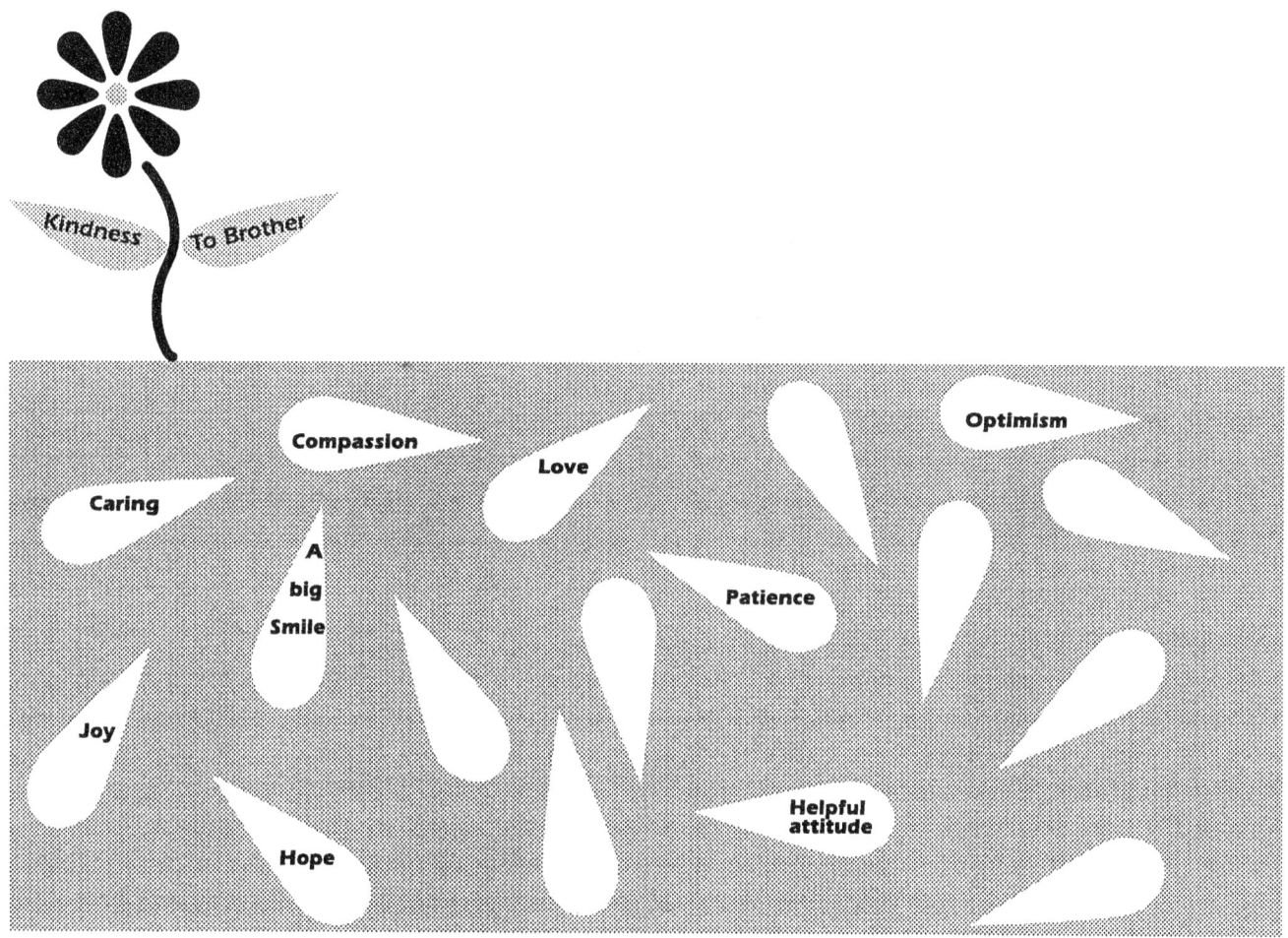

**Quiet Activity:** Close your eyes and go within. Take a few deep breaths and imagine... you and your friends planting peace-producing seeds. How do you feel as you put them in the ground? What are your hopes and dreams? How do you and your friends relate to one another as you plant these seeds of non-violence? What do you think of yourself for taking on this task? Imagine these seeds taking root and growing into the beautiful flowers, plants, and trees you drew above. See your world as peaceful as you can imagine. When you are finished, open your eyes, stretch... and begin planting those seeds today!

# 28

# NURTURE YOUR SEEDS OF PEACE

**Directions:** As you know seeds need care and proper attention if they are to grow into strong, healthy plants. Your seeds of peace also need important nurturing.

**Below you will find two columns: Peace Seed and Nurturing Action.**

* List the seeds you have planted in the previous **Peace Tool** and then think of an action you can take that will help bring that seed into life. Two examples have been done for you.

* When finished, share your answers with others and discuss how everyday little actions we take can grow into mighty deeds of accomplishment to benefit a lot of people!

| **Peace Seed** | **Nurturing Action** |
|---|---|
| compassion | think about how to be forgiving of people who hurt me |
| caring | take time out to visit my Grandma |
| | |
| | |
| | |
| | |
| | |
| | |
| | |

**Quiet Activity:** Close your eyes and go within. Take a few deep breaths and imagine... you are doing one of those nurturing activities. See yourself as vividly as possible. See the other person or people involved. How are you all feeling? Where is your attention? What is most rewarding about taking this little action? What do you think you will do next? Take your time and see the picture clearly. When you have finished, open your eyes, stretch and when you are ready, fill in the blanks below:

**Three actions I can take this week to nurture peace in my life are:**

1. 
2. 
3.

**Peace Tool # 5**

# WRITE A PEACE PROFILE

## Directions:

* Research (in books, magazines, on the Internet, or through conversations with people in your community) a person who has done something significant to promote peace. The person could be someone famous like Gandhi or Martin Luther King, or someone less famous, such as a mother who started a club for kids to get them off the street or a man who dedicates his life to saving boys from gangs, a kindly police officer, a sports coach.

* After you have some information on the person's life write a "Peace Profile" similar to the example done for you below. If the person is alive and in your neighborhood you could interview him or her!

* Collect copies of other teens' peace profiles and compile them into a folder or notebook. Read them when you need encouragement. Share and discuss them with friends or family members for inspiration. Talk about them with younger children. Honor these peace activists by modeling your actions after them.

**Example of Peace Profile** (information from *The Seattle Times Magazine*, 9/14/97)

Floyd Schmoe of Seattle, WA is 101 years old and has been nominated for the Nobel Peace Prize three times. He still hopes he gets it! Mr. Schmoe has written 14 books, many about peace. During World War I he carried wounded soldiers off of battlefields and during World War II he helped evacuate the Jewish people. After the bomb was dropped on Hiroshima and Nagasaki he took volunteers there to help rebuild houses. A few years ago at age 95, he created the Seattle Peace Park where people can go to think quietly about peace and how to become more peaceful. Mr. Schmoe is still involved in projects to reduce violence in society—his latest being—finding ways to help young girls in Bangkok who have been sold into prostitution.

Here are some questions you can discuss with friends or family when you are finished with your **Peace Profile**:

* What do you admire most about this person?

* How is he or she peace-smart?

* Who benefited the most from this person's actions?

* What can we all learn from him or her?

* What does he/she inspire you to do? to become?

**30**                                                         `Peace Tool # 6`

# YOUR PERSONAL PEACE STRATEGIES

**Directions:** What do you say to yourself about the violence you see in society? Would you consider yourself hopeful about this problem? How do you personally create more peace in your life and the lives of others?

**Below is a list of possible Peace Strategies.**

* Read each one, then place a check in the box which applies to you.

* When you are finished, review your answers, discuss them with a trusted friend, and reflect on the ones you'd like to do more often.

* On the lines at the bottom of the page, write your favorite **Peace Strategy**!

| **Peace Strategies** | Yes | Some-times | No |
|---|---|---|---|
| 1. I do little acts of kindness to help make the world more peaceful. | ❏ | ❏ | ❏ |
| 2. I try hard to listen when someone expresses an idea I don't like. | ❏ | ❏ | ❏ |
| 3. I believe that each person can make a difference to make the world more peaceful. .............. | ❏ | ❏ | ❏ |
| 4. When I read about or see violence in the media, I try to remember that there are many more non-violent people in the world than violent ones. .............. | ❏ | ❏ | ❏ |
| 5. If I know someone who is heading for trouble, I do something about it. .............. | ❏ | ❏ | ❏ |
| 6. I read something hopeful and uplifting on a regular basis. ........ | ❏ | ❏ | ❏ |
| 7. I believe that problems can be solved non-violently and I tell others that. .............. | ❏ | ❏ | ❏ |
| 8. I encourage others to control their tempers. .............. | ❏ | ❏ | ❏ |
| 9. I know that the police are there to help people and save lives. . | ❏ | ❏ | ❏ |
| 10. If I had the opportunity, I would work with police or other adults toward peace. .............. | ❏ | ❏ | ❏ |
| 11. I am developing skills and talents so that I can lead a non-violent lifestyle. .............. | ❏ | ❏ | ❏ |
| 12. I can usually be counted on to lend a listening ear to a friend with a problem. .............. | ❏ | ❏ | ❏ |
| 13. I try to steer young kids away from thinking that violence is "cool." | | | |
| 14. I take out my frustrations through some type of physical release like sports, dancing, or jumping rope. .............. | ❏ | ❏ | ❏ |
| 15. I have hope that I will have a bright future. .............. | ❏ | ❏ | ❏ |

**My favorite Peace Strategy is:**

**Peace Tool # 7**

# COMMUNICATING CLEARLY WITH YOURSELF

**Directions:** How clearly do you communicate with yourself? Have you ever really thought about what you say to yourself, inside your head?

Thoughts are powerful. In fact, brain researchers tell us that thoughts are the plastic material upon which we build our entire reality. Some scientists will go so far as to say that **our internal thoughts actually determine our external reality.** Not sure how this could be? Why not do the following experiment and see for yourself!

## Step 1: Keep track of your thoughts.

Watch yourself. What are you saying to yourself that could cause concern, worry, unrest, anxiety? For instance, are you saying: "This is an impossible situation." OR "It's tough right now, I think I'll go and talk to the school counselor."

* Place your thoughts into two categories: Thoughts That Hinder and Thoughts That Help. Are you tearing down or building up most of the day?

* At the end of the day, review your thoughts. Which thoughts have brought you the most unrest? Which thoughts have brought you the most peace?

* Before you go to sleep, change your hindering thoughts into helping thoughts. Go through your worries and concerns and restate your thoughts about your problems in ways that will bring you (and others) peace.

## Step 2: Keep track of your reality.

What is working in your life? What needs some adjustments?

* Watch how your thoughts affect your actions. Watch how your thoughts affect how other people respond to you.

* Pay extra close attention when you change a hindering thought into a helping one. How does your life change?

* What happens in your life as you consistently do this for a week or two? What changes are occurring inside yourself?

## *Continuation* COMMUNICATING CLEARLY WITH YOURSELF

### Step 3: Hold gentle, but firm, conversation with your negative mind.

The negative mind, the part of the mind that hinders us, is like a little kid who doesn't have all the information. It needs our help to maintain a positive attitude so it can enjoy life more. And like a child, it needs (and wants) boundaries. When you see that your negative mind is controlling what you think, talk to it as you would a child. If you are afraid of flunking a test, for instance, here are some things you could say:

*   OK. I hear that you are worried and scared.

*   You are forgetting that I know how to relax now when I take tests and I want to remind you that I did study for this one.

*   Let's just take a few deep breaths and think positive!

OR , if there is a more serious problem... an approach could be...

*   Yes, I know you think running away from home is a solution.

*   That is a rash action and could cause a lot of other problems. Like—How will I support myself?

*   Let's talk to the school counselor and explain what's going on.

**The goal here is not to let your negative mind rule your actions. Gently focus on helping thoughts and ways that will work *for you* and not against you!**

### Step 4: Use a journal to write down any hindering thoughts.

This can be very interesting because the more you write down negative thoughts, the more you will learn how to change them into helping thoughts. Try writing what ever comes to your mind for 10 minutes each day. Re-read what you have written. Change the hindering thoughts to helping thoughts. Pretty soon, you'll be writing only helping thoughts!

What do you want to happen in your life? Use your thoughts to create the exact life you want... and don't give up—not until you have changed every negative whisper. And... be prepared for many exciting discoveries... about yourself and your new world!

# GUIDELINES FOR COMMUNICATING CLEARLY WITH OTHERS

**Directions:** Take a look at the three basic elements involved in communication.

# The Messenger        The Message        The Receiver

**Now, consider that communication involves the following four steps.**

**Step 1:** The messenger forms an idea/s he or she wants to convey.

**Step 2:** The messenger puts the ideas into words and sends (talks, writes) the message to the receiver.

**Step 3:** The receiver gets the message and interprets it inside his or her own head.

**Step 4:** The receiver gives feedback to let the messenger know he or she has understood the message.

## Activity 1

Think about and discuss the following with a partner or in a small group:

* Give examples from your personal experience when you gave a message and the person who received it didn't understand it.

* Give examples when you were the receiver and you misinterpreted the message.

* Discuss how communication can break down during any of these four steps. What could go wrong?

**34** | **Peace Tool # 8**

*Continuation*

# GUIDELINES FOR COMMUNICATING CLEARLY WITH OTHERS

## Activity 2

With your partner or in your small group, read the following and give your own opinions and ideas along the way.

To maximize clear communication and to minimize communication breakdowns, try the following:

### When you are the messenger:

*   Maintain good eye contact with the other person.

*   Use clear, concise language as much as possible.

*   Disclose your own feelings, as well as your thoughts.

*   Encourage questions, comments from the other person.

*   Give the person time to think about what you are saying. Don't rush them to respond.

*   Keep your voice calm when you are upset.

*   Keep hostility, judgment, blame, and criticism out of the conversation.

*   At all times show respect for the other person, even when you disagree.

### When you are the receiver:

*   Maintain good eye contact with the other person.

*   Use clear, concise language as much as possible.

*   Disclose your own feelings, as well as your thoughts.

*   Encourage questions, comments from the other person.

*   Give the person time to think about what you are saying. Don't rush them to respond.

*   Keep your voice calm when you are upset.

*   Keep hostility, judgment, blame, and criticism out of the conversation.

*   At all times show respect for the other person, even when you disagree.

**Peace Tool # 8**

*Continuation*

# GUIDELINES FOR COMMUNICATING CLEARLY WITH OTHERS

In addition to the same skills needed for the messenger, the receiver has another very important job to do. That is, to be an active listener...

## An active listener...

* Shows interest in what the other person is saying by nodding, moving forward, and asking questions.

* Does not interrupt the messenger.

* Sits still and concentrates on what the messenger is saying.

* Listens hard for the unspoken ideas or feelings and states them back to the messenger.

* Summarizes what he/she thinks the message is so that the messenger will know it has been received properly.

## Activity 3

Go back to ways you have experienced communication breakdowns in the past Discuss the following with those in mind:

* Which of the skills listed above would have helped you out?

* Which communication skill/s will you practice today?

* How do these communication skills make you more peaceful?

* How do these communication skills make the world more peaceful?

# PRACTICING GOOD COMMUNICATION SKILLS

**Directions:** Good communication skills are developed through practice. For most of us, we will be learning and refining our communication skills throughout our entire lifetime. Begin now to use good communication skills and observe how much easier relationships can be!

Below are three of the most important communication skills to master:

* Reflecting Back Ideas and Feelings

* Asking Clarifying Questions

* Summarizing What Has Been Said

With a partner, take turns practicing them.

## Reflecting Back Ideas and Feelings

When the messenger is speaking it is sometimes apparent to the listener that there are powerful unsaid ideas and feelings. The messenger is often unaware of this. It's the listener's job to let the messenger know, in a gentle way, what is being left unsaid. Consider this example:

**Messenger:**  I don't get it. My little brother gets all the attention just because he is afraid of the dark. If you ask me, I think he's faking it!

**Listener:**  It sounds to me like you resent your little brother getting so much attention. Are you jealous?

## Person A reads each situation out loud and Person B tells what is left unsaid.

* I keep telling Candy to leave me alone. Why won't that loser know I am not her friend anymore? She just can't take it.

* Can you believe that our team is going to the state championship? This is like a dream come true!

* My mom told me I couldn't go; then my dad told me I could. I told them, What am I a yo-yo or something?

* When we have company, I can't act like myself. My parents expect too much out of me!

* My Mom just found out that she has to leave her job. Can you believe it! After she has been there over 10 years!

# PRACTICING GOOD COMMUNICATION SKILLS *Continuation*

* How many times do I have to wave my hand in class to get this teacher's attention? She is biased toward girls, I guess.

* Every time the telephone rings, I think, It's Tom (Tammy) calling to ask me for a date.

## Using Clarifying Questions

When something is not understood, it's important to ask clarifying questions to gain more information. Also, asking these questions, encourages the messenger to keep talking and shows that the listener wants to hear what is being said.

Some possible clarifying questions include:

* What are more of the details? (Who? What? When?) I'd like to hear more.

* You skipped over that pretty fast. Can you say that again more slowly?

* What else happened?

* What was your reaction? How did you feel?

* Is there anything else you need to say about this situation?

* Can you say more about that?

* I'm unclear about _____. Please repeat that idea.

## Person A reads the following statements. After each, Person B asks clarifying questions until the "whole story" is revealed.

* My Dad came home real late last night.

* Jimmy is always getting A's in chemistry.

* I am really feeling great right now.

* You'll never guess who visited us yesterday!

* I read a good book last month.

* Next week will be so important.

* Who knows? Maybe I will take a foreign language class.

**38**

## Continuation PRACTICING GOOD COMMUNICATION SKILLS

### Summarizing What Has Been Said

Sometimes what the messenger said is not what the listener received. When this happens, the conversation does not help forge bonds between people. Rather, the conversation causes frustration and can lead to mild, or even serious misunderstandings. It is a good habit to summarize what you have heard after the message is delivered. Some ways to begin a summary are:

* Let me understand what you have just said...

* I think this is what you have said. Correct me if I am wrong...

* I want to tell you what I just heard...

* Just a minute, before you continue I want to make sure I understand what you are saying...

**Person A talks about each situation for one or two minutes. After each, Person B summarizes the main ideas to make sure he/she has heard correctly.**

* You are excited about going to summer camp.

* You have just been told that you need to clean your room before going out.

* You are tired of always having to baby-sit your little sister.

* You drove to school and someone you are mad at wants a ride home with you.

* You are looking forward to your volunteer work at the local child care center.

**Peace Tool # 10**

# GUIDELINES FOR CONFLICT RESOLUTION

**Directions:** Most conflicts occur when one person is trying to get the other person to lose in some way. Conflicts cannot happen if the people involved think: WIN-WIN.

## Below are some effective ways to handle conflict.

Read or discuss them with a parent or friend. Then use them, along with the communication skills you learned in the previous **Peace Tools**, and watch how peaceful you're life can become!

When you are in conflict with someone...

*   Be open to working it out. Show the other person your willingness to make peace.

*   Define the problem together. Agree on what you are in conflict about!

*   Agree that both people will need to change. It is not one person's fault more than the other person's.

*   Make sure that you give yourselves plenty of time to work it out. If one session is not enough, agree to meet as many times as it requires to come to an agreement.

*   State your feelings without blaming the other person. Use "I" statements. That is, begin your sentences with the word, "I" and not "you."

*   Listen actively to what the person is saying. Ask clarifying questions. Use all the clear communication skills you know.

*   If it is difficult for you or the other person to keep calm, have a caring adult present while you two discuss the conflict. Make sure you both feel safe at all times so you can work out the conflict peacefully.

*   Put yourself in the other person's shoes. Reverse roles and take on the other person's argument. How does that change your own position?

*   Discuss how your conflict began in the first place. It is a real conflict or just a misunderstanding borne of poor communication?

*   When you have resolved this conflict, what will you do next time to avoid a conflict?

# PRACTICING CONFLICT RESOLUTION

**Directions:** Many conflicts can be resolved smoothly, if the parties take the time to find out what the other person wants.

**Below are descriptions of conflicts.**

* Under each one, write what both parties want.

* Next, role play the situation with a partner, using the conflict resolution skills used in the previous **Peace Tool.**

* Then, write down the WIN-WIN situation you arrived at. The first one is an example for you.

## Conflict Situations:

Joan is waiting for an important call from her boyfriend. She is frustrated and starts yelling at her little sister, Sally. But Sally refuses to get off the phone:

**Joan wants:** to keep the phone line open in case her boyfriend calls.

**Sally wants:** to talk with her friend

**WIN-WIN Resolution:** Sally gets off the phone now if Joan will do her chores for her this evening. Sally will talk to her friend later.

Joe's house is for sale and his Mom insists he keeps his bedroom clean because there are people going through the house at all hours. Joe hasn't had time to clean his room this weekend because of ski school. He says he'll do it, but he can't find the time. He and his Mom start to argue.

**Mom wants:**

**Joe wants:**

**WIN-WIN Resolution:**

Harry needs a date for the senior prom and his friend, Bill wants to fix him up with his sister. Harry likes Bill's sister, but she is a few inches taller than him and he will be embarrassed to go to the prom with her. Bill isn't taking "NO" for an answer.

**Harry wants:**

**Bill wants:**

**WIN-WIN Resolution:**

## Peace Tool # 11

# PRACTICING CONFLICT RESOLUTION *Continuation*

## Conflict Situations:

The biggest party of the year is being given by Valerie. Jane has not been asked and she thinks the reason is that she refuses to let Valerie copy her homework. They have argued about this many times and Jane just doesn't think it is fair, especially since Valerie is really smart, just lazy.

**Valerie wants:** _____

**Jane wants:** _____

**WIN-WIN Resolution:** _____

_____

Pete upset the new kid at school, Tom, the one who bench presses 250. Tom told Pete to meet him after school, but Pete didn't show up. Now they are both inside the counselor's office. Tom is mad and feels disrespected. Pete is mad and feels intimidated.

**Pete wants:** _____

**Tom wants:** _____

**WIN-WIN Resolution:** _____

_____

_____

_____

_____

_____

**42**

# MATURE RESPONSES

## Directions: Consider the qualities of a mature person:

✳   A mature person is responsible in words and actions.

✳   A mature person cares that the world is a safe and caring place.

✳   A mature person not only helps him or herself, but also helps others, and society in general.

✳   A mature person uses communication and conflict resolution skills instead of physical violence or verbal abuse.

✳   Becoming **peace-smart means becoming more mature** and responding maturely when in potentially violent situations.

With a partner or in a small group, **read the examples below** and discuss the following questions for each one:

✳   Was the person's response mature? Why or why not?

✳   What communication skills could the kids have used? (Use Peace Tools 8 & 9 for help.)

✳   What conflict resolution skills could the kids have used? (Use **Peace Tools** 10 & 11 for help.)

✳   What would you have done in this instance? Why?

## The Examples:

Peter, age 8, wants to play football during recess. None of the other boys want to play as they are busy shooting baskets. Peter starts shouting and yelling, and then begins pushing one of the boys. He falls down and Peter punches him hard and runs off.

Sally, age 13, knows that her girlfriend's boyfriend has brought a gun to school. She has seen it with her own eyes. Sally knows that her girlfriend will get mad at her if she tells anybody so she keeps quiet about it.

# Peace Tool # 12

## MATURE RESPONSES *Continuation*

Tom, age 11, sees bruises on the arms and backs of the legs of the little first grader he is mentoring. Tom points this out to a teacher.

Jamal, age 15, sees a kid about 16 kicking a homeless man. The kid looks dangerous, so Jamal decides to cross the street and hurry home by a different route.

Karina, age 17, is noted for her beauty. One girl at school is envious of her and attacks her in the school bathroom with a knife. Karina's face is cut up real bad. She gets her friends together and vows revenge.

Josh, age 9, has to watch his baby sister, age 2, while his Mom takes a nap. His sister plays fine for awhile, but then keeps asking for ice cream and starts crying and wailing about it. Josh starts yelling at her, and feels like he could take her and shake her. Instead, he gets her ice cream, even though he knows his Mom will be mad at him for doing it.

Sue, age 14, spends a lot of time hanging out with boys in gangs. She is in love with one of them, but he has hit her more than once. Sue is afraid because now she is pregnant. She decides to go to Planned Parenthood for an abortion.

**Pick one of the situations above and write your mature response.**

_____
_____
_____
_____
_____
_____
_____
_____
_____
_____
_____
_____
_____
_____

**44**

# STOPPING VIOLENCE FROM GROWING

**Directions:** How we think about and respond to things that happen to us can either stop violence or continue violence. The goal is to be so aware of our thoughts and feelings that we take appropriate actions.

## Below are some things to do.

* Under each one, write down the thoughts and feelings that led to the action the person has taken. The first one is done as an example for you.

* Then with a friend or someone in your family, discuss your answers... And remember to congratulate yourself every time *you* do something to stop violence from growing.

Tom decided to forget about a kid who shoved him in the lunch line...

**Thinking it wasn't worth the effort. Feeling self-confident. Not needing to prove a point.**

Jim forgave his best friend who punched him during an argument over a baseball game...

Sally walked away from her older sister who was screaming and yelling at her...

DiDi decided to be patient while driving in traffic instead of swearing and getting angry...

Mark apologized to his mother after swearing and calling her names...

Rather than hold a grudge, Tim decided to stay friends with two boys who were sorry they teased him so badly...

Karen decided not to pay back Sally for stealing her boyfriend...

## Remember...

Your goal is to develop skills so you can be detached from potentially violent people or situations.

**Peace Tool # 15**

# PRACTICING INNER PEACE

**Directions:** Your state of inner peace is your contribution to world peace. It can be a big challenge to stay calm and relaxed throughout a busy day. But with practice and persistence, you can learn to remain centered and in control, no matter how stressful or chaotic external events may be.

## Below are some guidelines for practicing inner peace:

*   Choose the ones that most appeal to you and role-play and discuss them with a friend.

*   Imagine yourself in circumstances where these actions will be useful.

*   Act out these situations until you can feel your body and mind responding, until the Peace Guidelines can become "second-nature" to you.

## Guidelines for Expanding Inner Peace:

**Breathe Deep.** Take deep breaths, allow the in breath to fill your lungs, and when you let out air, let out the problems, concerns, or stresses. In your mind see them leaving you. As you take in new air, see yourself becoming more confident and calm.

**Learn what triggers you.** If someone honks at you while driving or yells at you—does that get you mad and raise your stress level? Or does too much homework make you irritable and nasty to be around? What takes away from your personal peace? A great first step in becoming Peace-Smart is to understand yourself and your own responses to stress. Ask friends or family members for feedback and let them support and encourage you in this venture.

**Accept what you can and can't change.** We all want to have the "perfect life." But there are many things in life that are totally out of our control to change and no matter what we do, we can't change them. Then again, there are lots of things we can do to make life the way we want it.

# PRACTICING INNER PEACE *Continuation*

\*   Examine your problems especially the ones that are causing you the most stress. List them on a sheet of paper and then put them into two columns: Can Change/Can't Change at the Present Time.

\*   For the problems you can change sees the guideline below.

\*   For the ones you can't change, practice letting go of them, gently reminding yourself that they are out of your control and you can relax about them.

**Make a plan for a stressful problem.** Remember, there are no problems. Look at them as challenges with solutions just waiting to happen. You can acquire more peace, just by taking action! Write down the problem as you see it. Then brainstorm ideas for solving it or for getting help to solve it. No matter how serious your problem, remember there is help available to you. You can become more peaceful just by reaching out and asking for help!

**List your action plan below:**

_____

_____

_____

_____

_____

_____

_____

_____

_____

_____

_____

_____

_____

_____

_____

_____

_____

_____

**48**

# LETTING OFF STEAM

**Directions:** How do you manage yourself before you blow? We all get frustrated. We all get angry. And we all have the capacity to lash out and hurt others. The key is to let off steam, before our emotions build up and get too big to control.

## Below are ways that people have found useful for letting off steam.

Check the ones you do or would like to do more often

❑   Get a whole bunch of pillows and punch them often.

❑   Pump iron.

❑   Run, jog, or walk briskly daily.

❑   Find a place out of the way and yell at the top of your lungs.

❑   Sing and whistle regularly.

❑   Hike out in nature or take a walk in a city park.

❑   Listen to and dance to loud music.

❑   Stretch.

❑   Play sports.

❑   Jump rope.

List other ways you have for letting off steam below. Discuss them with a partner or in a small group. Talk about what works best for each person and share your experiences.

_____

_____

_____

_____

_____

_____

_____

_____

_____

# PUT YOURSELF UP!

**Directions:** Putting yourself down is violence toward yourself. The more you do it, the more you can be caught in a downward spiral of feeling bad about yourself and then feeling bad about other people, too. Look closely at how you talk to yourself. What do you say that helps you? What do you say that hurts you?

**Below are self-statements that harm.**

* Turn each one into a positive one. The first one has been done for you as an example.

* When you are finished, pick one or two of the positive statements to practice saying to yourself often.

* Instead of putting yourself down, begin today to "Put yourself up".

**Inner talk that puts you down     Inner talk that puts you up**

I'm so stupid, I can't do anything. ...OK. I didn't get the grade I wanted. It's not the end of the world. I'll ask if I can do anything for extra credit.

I never do anything right. ................._____

I don't have what it takes. ..............._____

I'll never amount to anything. ........._____

I'm a loser, so what else is new? ....._____

I can't. .............................................._____

I won't. ............................................._____

So what's the use? ..........................._____

Who cares, anyway? ......................._____

I'm unlovable. Who can like me? ..._____

# ASSESSING YOUR SELF-CONFIDENCE

**Directions:** Becoming Peace-Smart means becoming confident in our ability to handle situations non-violently. Below is a Self-Confidence Scale.

* Read each statement and select the appropriate number which best fits your current level of confidence for handling that situation.

* When you are finished, discuss your answers with a partner or in a small group.

* What have you learned about solving problems non–violently?

## Self-Confidence Scale:

5    Feel I could handle this situation well without using any violent methods.

4    Might lose my temper.

3    Would lash out verbally.

2    Would hit, punch, or hurt physically.

1    Would lose total control.

_____ Your best friend has just gotten beaten up. You are enraged and want to get back at the thugs who did this.

_____ A teacher is trying to help you understand a math problem in class. He is patient, but a student makes a derogatory remark under her breath, which you hear. You feel humiliated.

_____ You are working part-time at a convenience store on the night shift. Several boys come in and start taunting an elderly man there. You really want to stop their harassment before it escalates.

_____ It's late, you are tired, and you need to get up early in the morning. A good friend knocks at your door, drunk, depressed, and wanting to talk. You are really peeved.

_____ You have watched your Dad hit, push, and shove your Mother one too many times. This time you are going to do something about it.

_____ While you are driving on the freeway, minding your own business, a jerk speeds by, cuts you off and gives you the finger. You feel your blood boiling.

**Peace Tool # 19**                                                                                   **51**

# FUEL YOUR PERSONAL POWER

**Directions:** Violent people are usually people who don't feel strong inside themselves. They have to use physical force and domination techniques to feel powerful. True personal power comes from within. There is a knowing that fuels security and self-respect.

**A person using inner power doesn't have to prove anything to anybody.**
He or she has deep conviction about personal abilities and actions. How do you fuel your personal power? How do you remind yourself that true power lies within?

**Below are ways to feel personally powerful, from within.**

∗    Place a check under Yes, if the technique works for you; a NO, if the technique doesn't work for you.

∗    When you are finished, discuss your responses with a partner or in a small group Choose the three best ways that work for you.

∗    Print them on a chart and keep them in your bedroom or in another convenient place to fuel your personal power everyday!

**Check the appropriate column:**                                                           **Yes**   **No**

| | Yes | No |
|---|:---:|:---:|
| I say to myself often that I am a good person. | ❏ | ❏ |
| I tell myself that I can do something when I think I can't. | ❏ | ❏ |
| I know that I have some talents. | ❏ | ❏ |
| I work hard to practice skills such as reading or sports. | ❏ | ❏ |
| I practice controlling my temper and understand the need to do so. | ❏ | ❏ |
| I know that I am a good person. | ❏ | ❏ |
| I feel like what I give to others counts. | ❏ | ❏ |
| I spend time by myself everyday to get my head together. | ❏ | ❏ |
| I have goals I am working toward. | ❏ | ❏ |
| I feel good when I accomplish something positive. | ❏ | ❏ |
| I work to have the best for myself and others. | ❏ | ❏ |
| I trust myself. | ❏ | ❏ |
| I appreciate all my good points. | ❏ | ❏ |
| I remind myself that my life has purpose and meaning. | ❏ | ❏ |
| I motivate myself to meet challenges. | ❏ | ❏ |
| I tell myself my life is important. | ❏ | ❏ |
| I remind myself that I am a person worthy of love and respect. | ❏ | ❏ |
| I consider myself a fairly confident person. | ❏ | ❏ |

## 52

# Peace Projects

# 1 Identify your inner strengths.

Personal peace means knowing your personal power. In this art project you will remind yourself of what you have inside yourself to resist violence and live a peaceful lifestyle.

✳ Find a box which you can decorate on the outside to symbolize your personality, your likes and dislikes, who you are to other people.

✳ Once decorated fill the box with images cut from magazines or pictures you have drawn or artifacts you have procured which stand for the inner strengths you have that help you be peaceful. For instance, if one of your inner strengths is to remain calm under pressure you might put in your box a picture of a serene lake which will remind you of this power within yourself.

✳ Once you have filled the box, share the contents with some friends and discuss how these inner strengths will help you maintain a peaceful lifestyle for the rest of your life.

# 2 Create your personal peaceful place.

Do you have a place to go where you can feel relaxed? Where you can think quietly without interruption? Where you can be left alone to daydream, write, or doing nothing, if you wish? Peaceful places can help us become more peaceful. Create a peaceful place in your home or find a place in a park or somewhere in nature that you can visit when things get too hectic in your life. You might want to take the following steps:

✳ Think about what the best place for you would be. What is your ideal peaceful place? What would be realistic for you to try to create?

✳ Find out what others have to say about peaceful places. Research what different architects consider calm, serene structures. Find books in your local library on, Feng Shui, the Chinese science and art of placements, which offers a defined way to set up personal space for harmony and prosperity. It been used for thousands of years!

✳ Once you have more ideas, talk with family members about what you want to do, if you are setting up your peaceful place in your home.

✳ Use your creativity and imagination to create a special space for yourself which will reflect your hopes, dreams, and commitment to a more peaceful world.

# Peace Projects

**3** **Create your personal vision of peace.**
* Do you want to be more at peace with yourself?
* Do you want to be more calm and relaxed when solving your problems?

Below are areas of your life in which you might like to make changes that will help you be more at peace with yourself. Take your time with this project. It may take you several weeks or even several months to complete. Below each one that applies to you, write on a separate sheet of paper or in a special notebook:

What you can **say** to yourself to be more at peace about the situation.
What you can **do** for yourself to stay calm and relaxed about the situation.

* Conflicts to resolve with friends

* Self-Image concerns

* Trouble at school

* Problems with parents

* Worries about brothers, sisters, or friends

* Threats from other people

* Concerns about the future

* Health problems

* Financial problems

# Chapter 3

# FAMILY PEACE SMARTS

Raising peace-smart children is challenging, given the cultural barometer of our times. Violence seems to be everywhere as we read the newspapers or turn on the TV. Never has modern society been so awash with such stark attention to violence—whether real crimes reported in the newspaper or imagined acts of horror put on the screen for our "entertainment." Constructive, non-violent and loving adult models for dealing with problems are harder to find.

Parents, while critically important to children under any circumstance, become absolutely essential for imparting prosocial behaviors and attitudes in a violent society. Yet, a significant number of children and teens are growing up in families that are poorly positioned to fully discharge their parental responsibilities.

Youth advocates, then, not only need to support youths, but the parents as well.

By using the **Peace Smarts Model**, educators and social workers addressing the needs of families can offer hope and a genuinely empowering process to those parents willing to learn it. Although all of the information in this book can be useful to parents, this chapter contains supportive materials designed especially for them.

* Peace Tools, # 20-26 can be used in workshop settings with parents—to inform, begin candid discussions, to offer alternatives. Also, parents can learn the **PEACE Smart Process** as outlined in Chapter 1 and enjoy creating a **Family Peace Project** with their children. Many of these Peace Tools can be sent home to parents as important information.

* Peace Tools, # 27-31 are addressed to youth as part of their involvement in a **Family Peace Project**. Changing their family situation by themselves is not a realistic task for teens, but teaching them skills to contribute to Family Peace is important. Unfortunately, some parents may be absent or unavailable and a "family" project may not be possible. In those cases, only the **Peace Tools** or **Projects** in this chapter which are deemed most appropriate by the adult facilitator should be used. However, it is our intention, that any youth wanting to make positive contributions to his or her family (no matter how the teen defines "family") should have the tools, guidance, and encouragement to do so.

# For Discussion

1. Why are parents such important role-models for their children?

2. Who is a family you admire? Why?

3. Who is a family you do not respect? Why?

4. What would be your "ideal family life?"

5. What are ways you can bring about positive changes in your family?

6. Who in your family is easy to talk with? What qualities make them easy to talk to? Who is harder to get along with? Why?

7. What do you do to make life easier for your parents?

8. How have you helped a brother or sister recently?

9. If you were (are) a parent, what are you going to make sure you do for your children?

10. How can people in a family learn to get along better?

11. How do you communicate your differences with your family?

12. Who is the family leader? How do you know?

13. Name all those you respect in your family (including yourself). Give the reasons why you respect them.

14. How does your family handle stress?

15. What would you do, if you could wave a magic wand, to help heal families who were experiencing violence?

16. What do you think society should do for those families?

17. If you could morph one thing about your family, what would it be?

18. What can you do to encourage a family member to act peacefully?

19. Give one thing you can do today to contribute to family peace-smarts.

20. How can you become a more peaceful problem solver in your family?

21. Where can you go in your home to relax and let go of stress?

22. What is the family's responsibility for helping kids deal with anger?

23. How can families in neighborhoods support one another in being peace-smart?

24. What would you like to see happen in your family or in the family of a friend?

25. What does this saying mean to you, "Home is where the heart is."

**56**

**Peace Tool # 20**

## USE NON-VIOLENT DISCIPLINE METHODS

# For Parents

Discipline is one of the greatest expressions of love we can give children. Without discipline, there is no foundation for kids to learn or to value themselves or others. Children and teens need and want boundaries from us. It can be really tough, though, especially after a stressful day, to "keep our cool." Many parents opt for spanking or a push or a shove as a last resort, but consider it a harmless way to control kids. But what are we teaching our children when we resort to physical, or even verbal violence, with them? Research points out that hitting or spanking, even when a parent is "in control," can be harmful. With this type of discipline, as children grow older, it becomes more and more difficult for them to learn self-respect and self-control. **Consider the following:**

1.  Children who are often spanked tend to be more quiet, less articulate, and more sullen.

2.  Spanking tends to create nervousness and slow down learning.

3.  Harsh physical and psychological punishment leads to social distance among family members. When social distance increases, honest communication decreases.

4.  Frequent use of physical punishment is strongly associated with the development of low self-image in children and teens.

5.  Violence begets violence. Physical punishment for fighting simply does not teach kids to stop fighting.

6.  Spanking is related to chronic passivity in children and they may become overtly aggressive in their teens.

7.  Children who are controlled through being spanked develop an overdependence on external control. They become followers, always dependent on the watchful eyes of an overseer.

## Below are some things you can do, depending on your situation:

*   Enroll in a parenting class to find out some simple, effective ways for handling the particular stage your child is going through.

*   Call a friend when you are feeling out of control before you take any action with your child.

*   Discuss your situation with a counselor, pastor, friend, and find out what resources are available to help

**Peace Tool # 20**

# USE NON-VIOLENT DISCIPLINE METHODS

* Stop worrying about what others think. If you have to carry a screaming two-year old out of the grocery store, so be it. If you have to walk away from a teen who is publicly humiliating you, so be it. The first and foremost thing you can do is to do what is best for you and your child in the moment and forget about how it might appear to others.

* Strive to be extra careful when you are tired or under more stress. Make time to take a hot bath or hire someone to take care of the kids so you can get a break. It's crucial that you take care of YOU to do the best for your kids.

* If you have trouble controlling your temper, find ways to get help. There are free resources just a phone call away. Often children are innocent targets of frustrations that have nothing to do with them. Do as much as you can to manage and control your life, and problems with disciplining your children will decrease.

* Bring issues that require discipline to a family meeting to discuss when tempers are not in the way. This is especially important during the teen years as the older kids get, the more they will test our boundaries. Reminding them of the household rules at a time when the dust is settled is more likely to result in cooperation.

* Make punishment a last resort. Try to frame it as a consequence. "You were late three times, so for the next three Fridays, you'll have to find your own ride. I can't give my car to a 17 year-old who is irresponsible. You can try again in three weeks to keep your agreements." Experts say that remaining calm, cool, and objective when dishing out the bad news will more likely be effective. Although that's easier said than done, it is usually highly respected by our teens when we do it.

* If you slip up and lose control and lash out physically or verbally, apologize to your child or teen as soon as possible, tell him or her that you regret the incident very much and reassure your child of your love. And GET HELP IMMEDIATELY... your child is worth it... and so are **YOU**!

"What to Do... When Kids are Mean to Your Child" (Elin McCoy, Reader's Digest Publisher, 1997) is a book with practical advice for how parents can help children deal with bullies. Suggestions include:

* Listen with empathy. Realize that a child is reacting without years of experience and perspective.

* Let your child know you are on his side and will help him figure out ways to handle the situation.

* Teach your child to make clear statements such as, "I want you to stop kicking me." Suggest that he or she walk in groups.

* If the problem becomes serious, talk to the principal. If your child is having problems with a particular bully, chances are other kids are, too.

**Peace Tool # 21**

# SET UP AN AFFIRMING HOME ENVIRONMENT

# For Parents

To affirm someone means to:

* accept them as they are
* encourage them, especially during difficult times
* let them know they are special and important... and loved
* acknowledge their right to be here
* build up their positive traits

When people feel affirmed, they also feel loved and respected, and they are more likely to act non-violently. Research points out that non-violence can be learned, but that it cannot be learned as a series of techniques unrelated to a non-violent environment. In other words, peace strategies and skills will only take root in an environment that is cooperative and affirming.

**Below are ways which make the home environment an affirming one for parents and kids.**

* After each one check the box which applies to your family.

* You may want to give this checklist to each family member, then discuss each others' perceptions of what is working in your household.

* Are there other things you can do to make your home environment more affirming?

---

## Parents...

☐ Show interest in and help with kids' schoolwork .

☐ Find time to talk with children each day.

☐ Ask questions of kids often.

☐ Have realistic expectations of their children.

☐ Use encouraging remarks instead of put-downs.

☐ Listen carefully to children's problems.

☐ Provide household rules and give reasons for the rules.

☐ Express delight and encouragement with children's' creativity.

☐ Strive to reduce family obligations in order to spend time together.

☐ Can be counted on when kids get in trouble.

☐ Express love often.

## Kids...

☐ Know parents are doing their best.

☐ Willingly do what is asked (most of the time).

☐ Like to have fun with the family.

☐ Appreciate parents.

---

## WE ARE ALL MIRACLES...

# For Parents

**Below you will find a part of a speech given to the United Nations by the late artist, Pablo Casals.**

* Read it first to yourself and reflect upon it.

* Then when you feel ready, read it aloud to your child/children and discuss it.

* The questions at the bottom of this sheet provide topic ideas for your discussion. Help your child understand the essence of the message Casals is trying to convey: The more we teach children about the value and beauty of each individual life, the more we will reduce violence in our society.

> **"**...The child must know that he is a miracle, a miracle that since the beginning of the world there hasn't been and until the end of the world there will not be another child like him. He is a unique thing from the beginning until the end of the world. Now, that child acquires a responsibility: 'Yes, it is true. I am a miracle. I am a miracle like a tree is a miracle. Now, if I'm a miracle, can I do a bad thing? I can't because I am a miracle... I am a miracle that God or nature has done. Could I kill? Could I kill someone? No, I can't. Or another human being (who understands) he is a child like me, can he kill me?' I think that this theory can help to bring another way of thinking in the world. The world of today is a bad world. And it is because they don't talk to the children in the way that the children need. **"**

## Questions for Discussion:

1. What is a miracle?

2. What does "unique" mean? How are you unique? What do you value about your uniqueness?

3. How does recognizing each individual's uniqueness make for a more peaceful world?

4. Why does Casals believe that a miracle can't do a bad thing? Do you agree? Why or why not?

5. Do you think people today value the sacredness of life? Why or why not?

6. What would you do to teach children so they wouldn't grow up wanting to hurt or kill someone?

7. Do you agree that the world of today is a bad world? Why or why not?

8. Do you agree that talking with little children like this will help them grow up to be more peaceful? Why or why not?

9. Why does Casals say that children need this kind of talk? Is there anything else you think children need to hear?

**(Note: Quotation above is taken from: The Peace Catalog, Duane Sweeney, ed., 1984.)**

**Peace Tool # 23**

## YOUR FAMILY'S PEACE PLAN

# For Parents

Helping children and teens become more peace-smart is something that is done one baby step at a time. A great way to model for our kids the values of non-violence and cooperation is to work with them as a team to create a **Family Peace Plan.** The plan could reflect your goals toward:

*   supporting one another in helping make your home more harmonious

*   parents' expectations of kids

*   kids' expectations of parents

*   learning more ways to control stress, anger, and anything else that gets in the way of living peacefully

*   taking the peace message out into the world

**Use the chart below as a starting point.** Once you fill it in, you or the kids may want to draw it on poster board, and put it somewhere in your house where you can all see it and refer to it often!

| Issues | Activities | | |
|--------|------------|---|---|
| | **For Parents** | **For Kids** | **Ways We Know Are Successful** |
| | | | |
| | | | |
| | | | |
| | | | |

## THE FAMILY MEETING

# For Parents

**Weekly family discussions** can be invaluable in helping children learn and practice peaceful ways to solve problems, skills for handling conflict, mediation techniques, active listening, leadership skills, empathy and compassion. Years of research points out that regular family meetings also help children develop their abilities to take responsibility confidently and take risks courageously.

Time is always at a premium in most households, but taking the time for family meetings is probably one of the most important things parents can do. It is equally important for children of all ages, but teens benefit greatly because regularly scheduled meetings provide:

*     *a consistent structure to address volatile issues*

*     *a safe environment for communication of deep feelings*

*     *a way to give teens a sense of security without smothering*

*     *a way to give parents control without overstepping teen's boundaries*

**Below are suggestions for making a Family Meeting most effective.**

Try one or two of them at first and then gradually introduce others as you and your children become accustomed to getting together like this on a regular basis.

**Schedule the meeting in advance and notify your children about it.** Many families find it helpful to schedule the next meeting at the end of each one. If you are just starting out, use family consensus in determining the frequency of meetings. For instance, one parent we know says once a month is quite enough with two teenagers; while a single parent friend with an 10 year-old daughter says meeting less than every other week makes life too chaotic.

**Make the meeting special in some way.** Sit in a circle, light a candle, serve dessert, open with a positive affirmation about each family member, read an inspirational quote at the end—whatever you and your children would like to do to mark this get-together time as special. Adding a ritualistic quality to the meeting helps considerably in children anticipating the structure and moves the meeting to a level of spiritual nurturance for all.

*Continuation* THE FAMILY MEETING

**Establish simple guidelines.** These are basic rules of conversation and courtesy:

*   create an environment of respect and emotional safety

*   look at the person who is talking

*   no interrupting once a person has begun talking

*   ask questions for clarification

*   paraphrase what others are saying, especially if you are confused

*   try to remain calm if someone says something that upsets you—your turn will come.

These types of guidelines could be printed out or put on the refrigerator to remind everyone. Prepare to remind kids a lot during the meeting, too!

**Prepare your agenda carefully.** Many families like to keep the agenda short—to two or three topics at the most and get the mundane things out of the way first—such as discussing coming schedules. Topics which require more time could follow, such as discussing Peggy's slacking off on chores, or preparations for a family vacation. Ending with positive affirmations, remarks about improvements in attitudes or behaviors, what parents are proud of their children accomplishing, helps all to leave the meeting on an upbeat note.

**Don't use every family meeting to discuss and resolve discipline issues.** Sometimes those are better handled with the child alone and not with siblings in a more public arena. In general, the more severe the discipline problem, the less likely a family meeting will work to resolve it with that particular child. However, a family meeting is definitely an appropriate place for everyone to discuss the impact they felt from the problem. Airing emotions, grievances, and sharing feedback all help children and teens in need of discipline learn the consequences of their actions on others and get them to think about how the next decision they make might affect another person.

**Make family meetings fun.** Varying the location of the meeting—at a picnic on a summer afternoon; in the kitchen around the table to eat the apple pie and ice cream, lounging in the living room with hot chocolate on a blustery fall day; right after cleaning out the garage as a family, etc. These will help children anticipate fun and excitement, and if you have established some ritual structure within the meeting itself, varying the place and circumstances add to feelings of security and comfort.

**Ask the kids to handle a topic periodically.** When you feel your child or teen can address an issue, let him. Perhaps he can research more efficient ways for recycling or come up with a better idea for a quick meal for busy evenings? The family meeting is a

**Peace Tool # 24**

# THE FAMILY MEETING *Continuation*

great place for kids to take on leadership roles. Encourage your children, often, to propose topics to be discussed, to bring up uncomfortable issues, and to stand up for herself, when appropriate.

**Remember that the family meeting is a way to build unity and harmony.** Keep your focus on this goal. Remember, children grow up to be peace-smart in a home environment which allows it. Your commitment to the family meeting will reap a rich harvest for both you and your children in the years to come.

## A Word About Communication During Family Meetings...

Teach children the basics of good communication. Discuss and practice the following...

* Maintain eye contact with the person you are talking to.

* Ask clarifying questions, when you don't understand.

* Reflect back the person's feelings. Pay close attention to the ideas and emotions that are left unsaid. Name them in a gentle way, so the person talking is aware of the powerful unsaid emotions.

* Summarize what you have heard the other person saying. Make it a habit to end the family circle time by going around the circle and having everyone summarize what was discussed.

## TRAITS OF A HEALTHY FAMILY

# For Parents

In her book, *Traits of a Healthy Family*, Dolores Curran lists fifteen traits compiled from her responses to a survey taken of 500 family specialists. Based on that list, the following is presented in order of perceived importance by the experts interviewed. Along with each trait are the "hallmarks" applying to that trait.

Share the list with your family. Discuss which ones you do consistently and the ones you would like to improve upon. Put the list on the refrigerator door! Refer to the traits often, as you build a more peaceful family environment!

## Traits of a Healthy Family

**1. The healthy family communicates and listens.**
The family: listens and responds; has control over television; encourages individual feelings and independent thinking; recognizes turn-off words and put down phrases; develops patterns of reconciliation.

**2. The healthy family affirms and supports one another.**
The parent or parents have good self-esteem; everyone is expected to affirm and support; the family realizes that support doesn't mean pressure; the family's basic mood is positive.

**3. The healthy family teaches respect for others.**
The family: respects individual differences; respects individual decisions; shows respect to those outside of the family; respects the property of others.

**4. The healthy family develops a sense of trust.**
The adults trust each other deeply; the children are gradually given more opportunity to earn trust; the family realizes that broken trust can be mended; parents as well as children are trustworthy.

**5. The healthy family has a sense of play and humor.**
The family: pays heed to its need to play; recognizes its stress level; doesn't equate play with spending money; uses humor positively.

**6. The healthy family exhibits a sense of shared responsibility.**
Parents understand the relationship between responsibility and self-esteem; the family realizes that responsibility doesn't mean perfection; the family gears responsibility to capability; responsibility is paired with recognition; the family expects members to live with the consequences of irresponsibility.

**Peace Tool # 25**

# TRAITS OF A HEALTHY FAMILY *Continuation*

**7.  The healthy family teaches a sense of right and wrong.**
Parents share a consensus of important values; the parent/s teach clear and specific guidelines about right and wrong; children are held responsible for their own moral behavior; the family realizes that intent is crucial in judging behavior; parents help children to live morally.

**8.  The healthy family has a strong sense of family in which rituals and traditions abound.**
The family: has a person/or place that serves as a locus; makes a conscious effort to gather together often; honors its elders and welcomes its babies; cherishes its traditions and rituals.

**9.  The healthy family has a balance of interaction among members.**
The family: does not allow work and other activities to infringe routinely upon family time; actively discourages the formations of coalitions and cliques within the family.

**10.  The healthy family has shared spiritual values.**
A spiritual core strengthens the family support system; meaning and purpose outside of themselves drives goals and ambitions.

**11.  The healthy family respects the privacy of one another.**
The family: looks forward to the teen and separating years; moves from a base of parental rules to the one of mutually negotiated rules; does not dole out respect according to age, sex, or any other criterion; respects fads, friends, confidences, room privacy, and time to be alone; lets go.

**12.  The healthy family values service to others.**
The family: is basically empathetic and altruistic; serves others in concrete ways; seeks to simplify its lifestyle; is generously hospitable; keeps its volunteerism under control.

**13.  The healthy family fosters table time and conversation.**
In the process of talking social relationships, attitudes, and beliefs are enforced.

**14.  The healthy family shares leisure time.**
The family: keeps its collective leisure time in balance; prioritizes its activities; prizes opportunities to spend time alone with individual members; controls television usage; plans how to use its time.

**15.  The healthy family admits to and seeks help with problems.**
The family: considers problems to be a normal part of family life; develops problem-solving techniques.

## THE IMPORTANCE OF GUN SAFETY

# For Parents

If your home is like half of those in our nation, your home has a gun. As a responsible parent and citizen, it's important to:

* **Make sure all guns you may have cannot be reached by anyone who should not use them, especially children and teens.**

* **Keep your ammunition securely stored where a child or any other unauthorized person cannot reach it.**

* **Talk to your child about guns.** Discuss their uses and history. Answer your child's questions honestly and openly. If you can't answer a question, contact a knowledgeable person for the answer. By removing the mystery surrounding guns, your child will be far less curious about guns, and more likely to follow safety rules.

* **Make sure your child understands the dangers of real guns.** Talk often about the problems of violence related to easy access to guns.

* **Make sure your child understands the dangers of thinking carrying a gun in "cool."** Discuss often the uses of guns and other weapons on television programs, movies, and video games. Explain that gratuitous violence can de-personalize violence and make hurting someone seem glamorous. Watch TV and videos with your child and point out sensitive portrayals of violence which show suffering in realistic ways and which evoke empathy and compassion.

(Note: Some of the above information was adapted from:

*Learn Gun Safety: An Important Message to Parents* from the National Rifle Association, 1992.)

**The Importance of Gun Safety:**
* On average, 14 American children are killed daily in firearm homicides, suicides, and accidents.

* Gunshot wounds are the leading cause of death for males, ages 15-24

* Guns are now used in 60 percent of all teenage suicides.

From: *Safe by Design: Planning for Peaceful School Communities*, Sarah Miller, et. al., editor

**Peace Tool # 27**

# BEING A RESPONSIBLE FAMILY MEMBER

## Directions:

Response-Ability is the ability to respond maturely in any given situation.

* How do you respond at home to requests made of you?

* Do you know that you are a needed, integral part of what happens?

* Do you understand the importance of your contributions?

* Do you know that you make life easier for yourself when you make life easier for others, too?

Becoming **Peace-Smart** means you have responsibility to yourself and to others. And home provides a great place to practice.

### On the next page is a circle divided into four quadrants.

* In each quadrant write the words that most apply to you in that situation. Brainstorm with a friend, if you like, but put down the first words that come to your mind.

* Be honest with yourself and don't hold anything back. For instance, in the space marked "When I am given chores to do, I…" the first words that you write might be: don't like it, put them off, etc. That's OK. By being honest with yourself you'll know where there is room for improvement. After you write your answers in all four areas, be **responsible to yourself** and decide what changes you will make to be **more responsible in your family!**

# 68

## *Continuation* BEING A RESPONSIBLE FAMILY MEMBER

**When I am given chores to do, I...**

**When I see something that needs to be done around the house, I usually...**

**I would describe my responsibility at home as...**

**I think I am a responsible person because...**

## Peace Tool #28

# LIVING COOPERATIVELY

**Directions: Cooperation at home isn't always easy.**
Below are five ways that can make cooperation a little easier, especially when done regularly.

* In order to learn them well, you must first practice them. See if you can get a parent or brother or sister to take parts and role play the situations.

* If not, invite a friend to practice with you.

* After you are comfortable with a specific technique and you've role played it several times, try it out in real life. How does it feel to try something new? How does this new technique work in real life? How have you become more peace-smart?

* Choose one and practice it whenever you get the chance. Do you see your family becoming more cooperative because of your leadership?

1. **Express what you want in clear terms. Be thoughtful about what the other person wants, too.**

**Son and father are discussing loud music coming from son's bedroom.**

Son: I want to listen to this new CD all cranked up. I just got it and I like it better that way.

Father: I'm having a hard time concentrating on this work I need to get finished for my boss tomorrow.

**How can father and son resolve this situation to get both their needs met?**

2. **Express your feelings honestly and be willing to listen to the other person's feelings, too.**

**Two sisters, age 13 and 15 are arguing over a new magazine.**

Sister age 13: But it's my magazine, it was sent to me. So you can't read it.

Sister age 15: It was sent as a promotion, your not a subscriber. Besides, I'm older and I have every right to read it, too.

**How can these sisters state their feelings about wanting the magazine and help one another understand each other and work things out cooperatively?**

*Continuation* LIVING COOPERATIVELY

3.    Repeat back what the other person is saying so you understand it clearly before you respond to it.

## Mother and son, age 16, are discussing his curfew.

Mother: What I am trying to say...

Son: You can't make me stay home on weekends—I won't do it.

Mother: I'm not saying that, I just...

Son: I am telling you this it totally unfair...

Mother: If you would stop interrupting me, I'd like to explain...

**What questions can the son ask to understand what the Mother is really trying to say? How can he better contain his emotions until he has all the information?**

4.    Give encouraging remarks when you see someone needs them.

## Sister, age 14 and brother age, 11 are talking about school.

Brother: I just flunked my big math test. Boy, am I in trouble.

Sister: Well, you should have studied more.

Brother: I studied like mad, what do you mean?

**What could the sister say to the brother to encourage him instead of put him on the defensive?**

5. In conflict situations, put yourself in the other person's shoes.

## Two brothers, ages 12 and 16, are beginning to argue about their lost dog.

Brother age 12: You never did fix the gate like you said, now look what happened.

Brother age 16: And you didn't feed him. You never do that on time. Now he's run off in search of food and it's all your fault.

**What would happen if the brothers stopped blaming and got in touch with how the other one felt about their dog being gone? How would the conversation go then?**

# HOME IS WHERE THE HEART IS

## Directions: Considers these remarks:

A child, age 8, tells what peace is:
"Peace is people talking together with a heart in between them."

The great leader Gandhi explains nonviolence:
"Non-violence, which is a quality of the heart, cannot come by an appeal to the brain."

* What are the similarities in the messages of these two quotes?

* Does being heart-felt mean that we have to be mushy?

* Or are the qualities of the heart deeper and more meaningful the more we explore them?

## Below are a list of words, or qualities of the heart.

* Think about what each trait means to you.

* Then on the line next to it write what you could do at home to express that quality of heart to a family member.

* The first one is done for you as an example.

| kindness | Cook breakfast on Saturdays so Mom can sleep in. |
|---|---|
| patience | |
| courtesy | |
| respect | |
| love | |
| appreciation | |
| encouragement | |
| compassion | |
| forgiveness | |
| sincerity | |
| admiration | |
| gratitude | |

(Note: Quotations are taken from: *The Peace Catalog*, Duane Sweeney, ed., 1984.)

**72**

# MAKE AN APPOINTMENT— TO TALK PEACE!

**Directions:** Sometimes our problems with a person don't go away easily. We have anger or we resent something. We harbor grudges. We need to talk it out with the person, but are afraid of what might happen.

**Here's an idea that may work if you find yourself in such a circumstance.**
You can use it when having a problem with a family member or with a friend. Ask a friend to read you these directions while you do the exercise or you become familiar with it and do it on you own.

# THE IDEA!

**First:**

* Get in a comfortable position and close your eyes.

* Prepare yourself to spend some quiet time inside yourself by taking several deep breaths and stretch, if needed.

* See the person in your mind's eye as clearly as possible.

* Tell this person you want to make an appointment with him or her to discuss your differences.

* See the person responding positively, eager to get together with you.

**Second:**

* Stay in your imagination and see the two of you at your chosen location talking. Now is the time to tell that person everything you would like to. Let it all out. Don't hold anything back.

* See yourself saying everything you always wanted. See the other person listening very carefully, nodding, encouraging you to be truthful with your feelings. See the person understanding you in a way you could have only hoped for.

* Feel yourself relaxing as you begin to realize that he or she is really hearing you, cares about you, and is trying very hard to resolve the differences between the two of you. A great load is off your shoulders!

* Take several deep breaths and thank this parent, sibling, or friend for listening to you and for caring about you. You two are really connected again. Doesn't it feel great?

## Peace Tool # 30

# MAKE AN APPOINTMENT— TO TALK PEACE! *Continuation*

## Third:

* When you feel finished, open your eyes and slowly let yourself come back to the present.

* How do you feel now? Does making an appointment with this person feel as scary?

* Do you feel ready to make the appointment in real life? Or do you feel that you no longer even need to talk with this person—that once you vented your feelings, the problem went away?

## Remember...

Whatever you choose to do now, do it knowing that the person you are having difficulty with is human, just like you. Use what you learned in your imagination to make the situation better. And congratulate yourself on resolving a problem peacefully!

## Write your solution or draw a picture that makes your situation better:

**Peace Tool # 31**

# FORGIVE AND FORGET

## Directions: In this activity, you will try out two steps. 1. Forgive 2. Forget.

Even sometimes when we resolve our problems with others we still haven't forgiven them for what occurred.

## Forgiveness takes a lot of guts.

For most of us, it's very hard to do, especially when the person we are forgiving has hurt us deeply. Be easy on yourself and choose a situation that has a high probability for ending successfully. Good Luck!

## Step 1: Forgive

Think of a family member that you need to forgive. The process of forgiveness can take as long as you want. If you need to spend a week or a month thinking about it and going over it in your mind before you can bring yourself to forgive, do it. Look at the list below... Will it help you to...?

* Make an appointment with the person in your mind and do the exercise in Peace Tool #30, this time concentrating on what you are saying to forgive him or her

* Talk with a friend about it

* Talk with a professional about it, such as a teacher or a counselor

* Spend quiet time each night before going to sleep thinking about it

* List the qualities you like about the person

* List why you are grateful to have this person in your life

* Write down how you will feel inside once you have forgiven

* Let out your emotions concerning this person by writing in a journal for a few weeks

No matter what you do, remember you may or may not want to tell the person directly that you have forgiven him or her. That's up to you, but you sure will feel better, once you have forgiven the person in your heart!

**Peace Tool # 31**

# FORGIVE AND FORGET *Continuation*

### Step 2: **Forget**

* Once you have forgiven, you can let go of all the anger and any other feelings you have about the situation.

* This is critically important to do because if you keep churning it over in your mind, chances are, you are going to be right back where you started.

* All the work you did around forgiveness may be wiped out if you keep dwelling on the injustices that occurred.

* Every time you think about the incident, gently remind yourself that you are letting this one go.

* Forget and move on... and watch how your life transforms because of your courage!

## Write a letter or a poem about forgiving and forgetting:

_____

_____

_____

_____

_____

_____

_____

_____

_____

_____

_____

_____

_____

_____

_____

_____

_____

_____

_____

# Peace Projects
## For the Family

**1** **Show how your family is related to the human family.**
Draw a way to represent the following on separate sheets of paper:

* Your family

* Your school

* The block on which you live

* Your city or town

* Your state

* An outline of the United States

* An outline on North America

* The world

During a family discussion pick the drawing of your family and then choose one of the other drawings. Put the two papers side-by-side on the floor. Talk with family members about how peace in your family can help create peace in that larger environment. Some questions to consider could be:

* What do we do as a family that makes a difference to others?

* What are long-term effects of our peace-smart actions?

* How do we get peace in our world (town, continent, etc.) by being more peaceful at home?

* Do we take our responsibility seriously to help others become peace-smart? Why or why not?

* What would we like to do as a family to show others on our block (at church, school, in our town) that we are a family committed to peace smarts?

Spend several evenings putting different drawings beside the drawings of your family. What are you learning about the importance of family to help change the world? What have you learned about the connections between your family and the human family?

# Peace Projects
## For the Family

**2** Develop a Family Mission Statement which shows everyone's commitment to peace. **First:** Think and discuss: What is a Mission Statement? Some thoughts include:

\* It is a clear, succinct statement of the purpose of a group.

\* It is a statement everyone agrees on.

\* It includes those things which are of the highest priority for each group member.

**Second:** Brainstorm the attitudes and values that express peace in the world.

**Third:** Select those attitudes and values which your family can commit to, which are important enough to do something about.

**Fourth:** Write three or four sentences on how your family will support and express those values in your home and in the world.

**Your Family Mission Statement** could be shared with other families in your church group, school or community organization. Talk with others about your commitment to peace as a family. Perhaps enough people will be interested to write a Community Mission Statement!

**3** As a family mobilize other families in your neighborhood. Make up a petition for your mayor or other representative that you want an end to violence in your town. List what you think should happen immediately. Enlist the help of your family members to write, type, and duplicate the petition. Then the entire family requests that friends, neighbors, and community members sign the petition. Doing this activity as a family, shows your solidarity around the issue of violence and also models to others the importance of the family in promoting peace. When you have all the signatures you want, take the petition to City Hall, and present it to the mayor... as a family. Or better still, invite as many families who would like to, to show up and present a united front to the politicians. Parents and children take turns explaining why the issue is important, what you suggest be done about it, and why the mayor should take the petition seriously. Follow up several weeks later to make sure action is being taken.

# Chapter 4

# PEACE SMARTS
## at School

Adolescence is a period of turmoil and stress and many teens may "act out" their problems to varying degrees. In the past decade we have seen an increase of "acting out" violently at school. Reasons for the rise in school violence include: easy access to guns, increasing number of teens using alcohol and drugs, and students seeking thrills out of boredom. And even students who haven't been personally affected by school violence suffer. They are much more likely to be fearful and uncertain about pursuing their education in an unsafe environment.

The increase of crime at school has, of course, led to more and more intentional teaching about crime prevention. Since violence is a learned behavior, it can be unlearned. In this chapter of **Peace Smarts**, ideas and strategies are given which can assist students in preventing school violence and in establishing a positive school atmosphere. Working together in teams with adults is stressed here, for only when the adults truly listen to the kids will we be able to create schools which truly respond to their needs.

## Peace Tools in the following two categories are specifically designed to:

*   help with classroom cohesion and group dynamics, so that students understand that the foundation for peace smarts lies in caring and cooperation (Peace Tools, # 32-24)

*   explore the nature of peace and ways to prevent violence and adopt a peaceful way of life, especially at school (Peace Tools, # 35-39)

# For Discussion

1. How do you know when you are being compassionate? When someone else is compassionate toward you?

2. If you could make your classroom or school more compassionate, what would you do and why?

3. Do you feel safe at your school? Why or why not?

4. How does conflict usually start at school?

5. Do you respect the way school authorities handle conflicts or violent incidents? Why or why not?

6. What do you think could be (or should) be done at school to better deal with student violence?

7. Is dealing with violence the same as being peace-smart? Why or why not?

8. In what ways is being peace-smart more than merely coping with violence?

9. How would you define a "philosophy of peace?"

10. Who are proponents of peace that you have read about or actually know? What do you admire most about these people?

11. How do little things such as name calling, belittling people, teasing, etc. become hard to control at school?

12. Do you think it is important to pay close attention to changing these littlest "acts of violence" at school? Why or why not?

13. Describe a person at your school who is peace-smart. Is he or she respected by the other students, why or why not?

14. Is it cool at your school to be non-violent and pro-peace? Why or why not?

15. Is blame a problem at your school? How can it contribute to violent behaviors?

16. What do you perceive is (are) the biggest problem at your school related to violence: threats, gangs, guns, etc.? If you were in charge what would you do about these problems? What would your desired outcomes be?

17. How have your feelings of safety at school changed over the years? Do you feel more or less safe than when you were in grade school, for instance?

18. What contributes to people's fear of violence?

19. What can schools teach to help reduce that fear? What can schools teach to help create a non-violent society?

20. Is a non-violent society possible in your mind? Why or why not?

21. What is your personal vision of peace? How will you go about attaining it?

22. How will you go about helping other students at school become more peace-smart?

23. What responsibilities do schools have to raise peace-smart kids?

24. Can schools realistically be expected to deal with the problems of teen violence? Why or why not?

25. What is your most important responsibility at school for helping to "keep the peace?"

**Peace Tool # 32**

# CREATING A COMPASSIONATE CLASSROOM

## Directions: On the lines below:

*   Write the dictionary definition and your own definition of "compassion."

*   Then cut out the ideas below, put them in an envelope, and pull one out every day, for 5 days (or one week of school).

*   Meet with a small group of other students for 15 minutes every day, too, and share what you each have pulled. During this time discuss how you will all accomplish your "compassion activity" that day. Teachers, of course, are invited to join in, too!

## At the end of one week:

*   Have you noticed any changes in your classroom?

*   What happens when everyone does something for someone every day?

*   Is the classroom climate more caring and compassionate? How?

*   Do people know each other better?

*   Is there more respect present?

*   Are students having more fun?

As a class discuss these questions, along with your observations, with your teacher. Then formulate your class plan for continuing the compassionate acts for the rest of the school year.

**Compassion (dictionary definition)**

_____

_____

_____

**Compassion (your definition)**

_____

_____

_____

# CREATING A COMPASSIONATE CLASSROOM *Continuation*

## Activities to Foster a Compassionate Classroom

**Find a fellow student who needs some help with homework** or doesn't understand an assignment or a concept which you do understand. Help that person in class if there is time. Or make an appointment to meet with the person after school.

**Ask your teacher if there is anything you can do to help** him or her today. Be courteous and willing to do a favor.

**Be available to someone.** Ask your teacher if you can have a minute to stand up and say, "I am available today to listen to anyone who wants to talk about any problems they are having at school or at home. I will strive to be a good listener and offer you support." The first person who takes up your offer is the person you listen to. Don't strive to do anything about the problem, but if it is serious, such as your classmate is contemplating suicide, or knows someone who has brought a gun to school, talk with an adult at the school whom you trust.

Be attentive all day to people in your class in need of assistance. If your teacher needs help handing out papers, volunteer to do it. If a classmate looks like they could use a friendly smile or an encouraging word, step right up!

**Write your own definition of compassion** on the black (or white) board or on a sheet of paper that you will put up in your classroom for all to see.

**Help a student** that you are not real good friends with or who might be new to the school or someone you think just needs a kind word. Say something nice to this person today.

## Peace Tool # 33

# FOR THE GOOD OF THE WHOLE

**Directions:** Practice being a classroom community. Take a zero tolerance policy to violent behaviors.

## As a class go through the list below and decide:

* What is acceptable some of the time
* What is absolutely **not** acceptable anytime

## Then in the lines below:

* Write your own personal reasons for following the guidelines established by the class.
* Explain in your own words why these guidelines are for the good of the whole class and each individual student in it.

| Behaviors | Acceptable Sometimes | Zero Tolerance |
|---|---|---|
| Teasing | | |
| Calling People Names | | |
| Put-Downs | | |
| Cutting in line | | |
| Cursing, foul language | | |
| Laughing at someone | | |
| Judging other classmates | | |
| Speaking disrespectfully | | |
| Making fun of someone's answer in class | | |
| Ostracizing a classmate | | |
| Racial slurs | | |
| Distasteful jokes | | |
| Gossip | | |
| Answering back to the teacher | | |
| Criticizing someone | | |
| Sexual harassment | | |
| Pushing, Shoving | | |
| Hitting, Punching | | |
| Carrying or showing weapons | | |
| Using weapons | | |

# FOR THE GOOD OF THE WHOLE *Continuation*

**These guidelines are important to me and my classmates because:**

_____

_____

_____

_____

_____

_____

# 84

## WHAT ARE YOUR PEACE ETHICS?

**Directions:** The dictionary defines "ethics" as "a set of moral principles or guidelines."

Ethics can also be seen as codes of behavior or ways to live for good and noble purposes.

## What are your ethics concerning peace?

### In a small group or as a class:

* Brainstorm "A Code of Peace Ethics"

* Write them on the shield (see next page) to remind you that your peace ethics are a way to protect you from a violent lifestyle.

### Some ideas for you to write on your shield could be:

* Act with kindness.

* Control my temper.

* Have peace-smart friends.

* Help younger kids stay out of trouble.

Color your shield, cut it out and paste it in your notebook or some other place where you will see it often.

# WHAT ARE YOUR PEACE ETHICS? *Continuation*

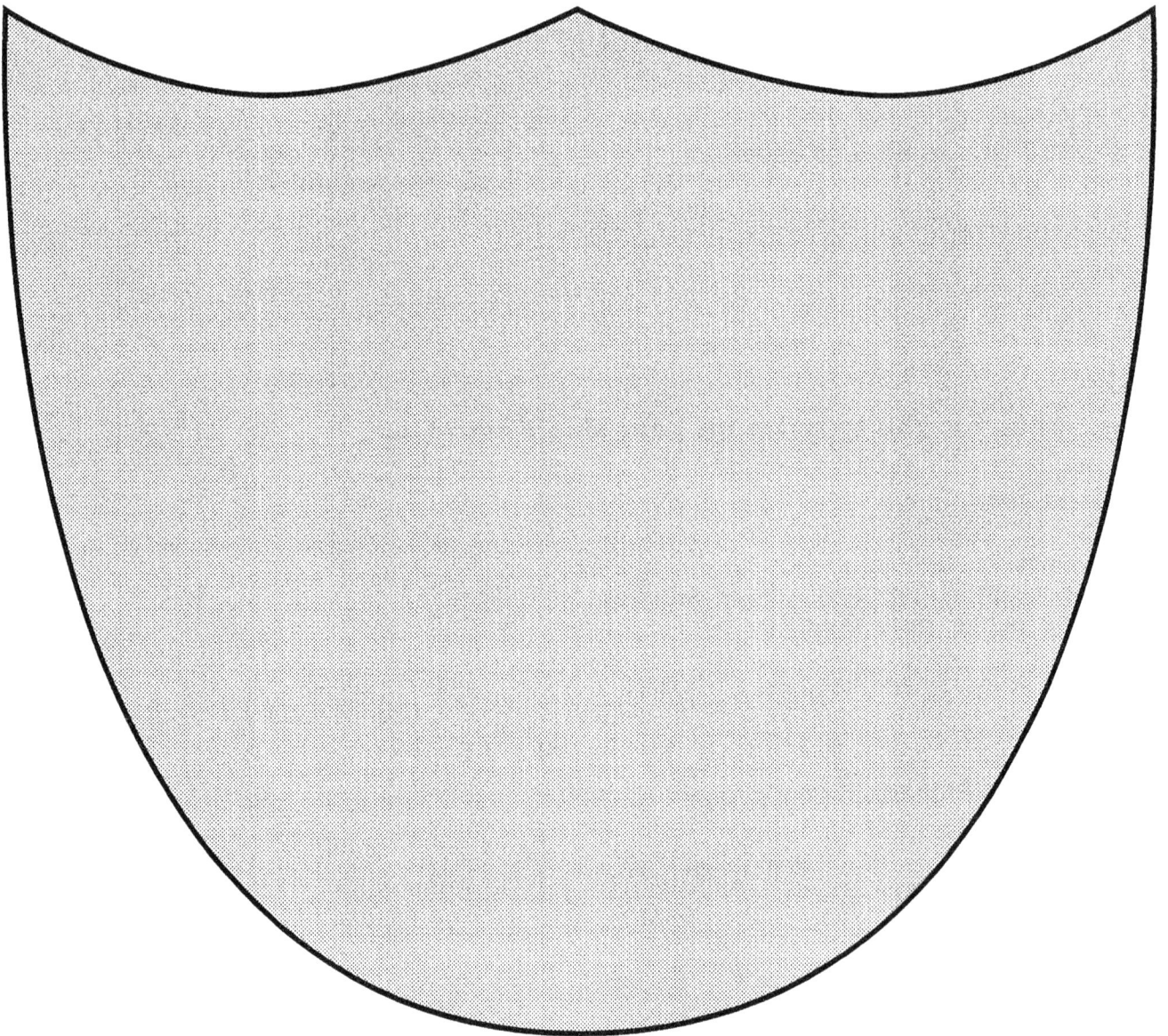

# SYMBOLS OF PEACE

**Directions:** Symbols of peace have been prominent in many societies, dating back thousands of years. In this Peace Tool you will have an opportunity to think about and discuss things that stand for peace.

## In a small group or with one other person:

*   Read the list below and in the space next to each symbol tell why you think the object does (or does not) represent peace well.

*   Then discuss the questions to explore more ideas. (If you want, you can research the origins of each symbol to know why it evokes peace and how it has been used over the years.)

**Peace Symbols**                          **A Good Peace Symbol?**

a white dove alone or with an olive branch    _____

hippie peace symbol                           _____

handshake                                     _____

waving a white flag                           _____

the word, "shalom"                            _____

Two fingers in a "V" formation                _____

peace treaties                                _____

raising arms and hands                        _____

## Questions to think about and discuss:

1.   What are other symbols for peace that you have seen or read about?

2.   How do peace symbols help us?

3.   If you were to invent a new peace symbol that could be understood internationally, what would it be?

4.   What would be a good peace symbol for your school to remind kids to stay peace-smart?

5.   Can you think of ways to get this symbol:

    *   accepted by the student body?

    *   seen in popular places at school?

    *   discussed about in classes?

    *   used to help bring more peace to your school environment?

**Peace Tool # 36**                                                          *87*

# WHAT IS NEEDED FOR PEACE?

**Directions:** Geoffrey Canada is a youth counselor who has worked in the inner city for over 20 years, helping kids stay away from a violent lifestyle.

Below are quotes from his book, *FistStickKnifeGun: A Personal History of Violence in America* (Beacon Press, 1995).

* Read each one, then in the space below it, write what you think about his opinion and whether you agree or disagree with it.

* After you are finished, compile a list of what you think are the most important things needed for living a peaceful way of life.

* Can you work with other kids at your school to bring these things into your lives and the lives of others? How?

## What do you think about the following ideas?

"When dealing with the issue of young people and violence in our country, it's clear that we can't separate violence from all of the other problems that plague our youth: educational failure, teenage pregnancy, drug and alcohol abuse, lack of employment, crime, AIDS... the list goes on and on." (p. 137)

_____

_____

"... our children need to learn the same skills that are taught to UN peacekeepers." (p. 147)

_____

_____

"Safety plans are a crucial element to making peace. These plans are necessary because adults often pay little or no attention to where violence is likely to occur in schools or after school programs. But children know. Children know where fights happen, and why those places are chosen. While this information is common knowledge among children, adults never ask *them* how to reduce or prevent violence. We go about hiring security guards or bringing in metal detectors, with no thought that children can tell us much of what we need to know about violence reduction." (p. 148)

_____

_____

# 88

## *Continuation* WHAT IS NEEDED FOR PEACE?

"... making peace is difficult for children who have grown up fighting enemies real and imagined every day they can remember." (p. 157)

_____

_____

"Part of what we must do is change the way we think about violence. Trying to catch and punish people after they have committed a violent act won't deter violence in the least. In life on the street, it's better to go to jail than be killed, better to act quickly and decisively even if you risk the certainty of being caught." (p. 159)

_____

_____

"And don't be fooled by those who say that these teenagers will never work for five dollars an hour when they can make thousands of dollars a week (dealing drugs). I have found little evidence of this in my years of working with young people. Most of them, given the opportunity to make even the minimum wage, will do so gladly." (p. 162)

_____

_____

"I believe all handgun sales should be banned in this country." (p. 165)

_____

_____

After thinking and writing about Mr. Canada's ideas, I think the following things should be done at my school, starting today:

1. _____
2. _____
3. _____
4. _____
5. _____

**Peace Tool #37**

# THE WAY OF PEACE

## Directions: Think about these questions:

* Is violence inevitable?

* . Is fighting and aggression so built into humans, that it can't be stopped or changed?

* What about the individuals that are able to control their impulse to violence?

* How are they different? What have they done to overcome anger, rage, or feelings of powerlessness?

An interesting man, Menchu, was a Quiche Indian who survived the torture and slaying of several family members in Guatemala, yet never sought revenge through violence. He won the Nobel Peace prize.

Find out more about Menchu or research a person who has lived a life dedicated to peace. Read about this person's life, then complete the ideas below about this person:

## A person who lived a way of peace is: He or she...

overcame difficulties by... .

_____

kept themselves under control by...

_____

thought that the important things in life were...

_____

took care of themselves by...

_____

took care of others by...

_____

expressed their inner power by...

_____

_____

After examining this person's life, use the lines below to write the best way of peace for _you_ right now at this time of your life.

_____

_____

**Peace Tool # 38**

# HANDLING INTIMIDATION

**Directions:** Some kids think the way to be powerful is to have power OVER people. They threat, intimidate, and scare others.

Are there kids doing this at your school? Are there kids who feel afraid and who can't relax at school?

*    Below are things you can do about this problem.

*    Pick one or two and discuss with friends and a teacher ways they may work at your school.

1. **Create a ZERO Tolerance Policy for any type of intimidation**. This means that the teachers, administrators, and school board have a written policy about intimidation and that the students know the consequences if they try to intimidate others. If your school doesn't have such a policy, maybe you are the student to get it started? If your school does have one, has everyone read it and understands it?

2. **Help your school environment be a positive and affirming one**. What can you and other kids do to help boost student body self-respect? For instance, you could conduct a campaign to eliminate a victim mentality and replace it with assertiveness and self-confidence. Or you could design a series of school-wide assemblies to motivate and generate a spirit of appreciation and cooperation. Get together with others and put on your thinking caps and use your leadership skills. Don't let the intimidators run your school!

3. **Invite caring adults in authority to have a regular presence at your school**. Police and security guards are usually present in most schools having difficulties. Can you invite others to join them? For instance, are there fathers in your neighborhood who could take time to be at school every day for an hour on a rotating basis? Are there community service volunteers, sports figures, ex-gang members who could speak at lunchtime on a regular basis? Look around your community for adult help and discuss ways these adults can get to know the intimidators and guide them toward better choices of behavior.

4. **Provide forums where students can discuss the problems and come up with solutions.** Do those who are being threatened have a safe place to express themselves without fear for their safety? Do these kids feel comfortable talking with someone who can help them? Does your school provide services for mediating conflicts and/or teaching kids how to resolve communication problems without violence? You and your friends could be instrumental in starting important meetings so that all those concerned can discuss the issues face to face and come up with ideas to try out.

## Peace Tool # 39

# ADULTS CAN HELP

**Directions:** Do kids at your school know where to go to get help? And just as importantly, do they feel safe in seeking adult help?

Below are things that you or someone you know could do if dealing with a potentially violent problem.

Check the ones you would feel comfortable doing if you were facing such things as:

* knowing who was bringing a gun to school

* being part of a group that was continually harassed by gang members

* being afraid a friend was planning suicide, or some other very serious problem

| Possible Actions | Would Feel Comfortable Doing |
|---|---|
| Talk with a teacher at the school. | ❏ |
| Talk with one of the school counselors. | ❏ |
| Talk with the principal or a vice-principal. | ❏ |
| Seek help from a school security guard. | ❏ |
| Discuss the matter with one of my parents. | ❏ |
| Discuss the matter with a parent of a friend. | ❏ |
| Ask help from the police. | ❏ |
| Call a local teen help hotline. | ❏ |

Now look over your list. Which ones are you not comfortable doing? Why? What needs to change before you would be comfortable taking those actions?

On the lines below, write the phone numbers of those adults you want to call in case you need help. Cut out the bottom of this page and keep the numbers safe, where you can reach them in a hurry, if needed.

Three adults I would feel comfortable turning to in case of trouble at school are:

| Name | Phone Number |
|---|---|
| 1. | |
| 2. | |
| 3. | |

# **Peace Projects**
## For School

**1** **Make a classroom "morph-violence" box.**
In it kids can put slips of paper on which they have told of violence in their lives and how they have morphed it into peace. Success stories. Or they could explain about a violent situation that they would like help with. Before you get started discuss the purpose of the box and the integrity that is needed to make it work. Make sure everyone in the class knows how to use it. Talk about the pros and cons of having morph-violence boxes around the school. Would they help your school become more peace-smart? Would the students take advantage of them? Why not put one in the lunchroom to see how students respond to it? On the first day, explain to the kids why it is there and who will be reading the slips of paper and what will be done with them. For instance, if students are sharing their stories about becoming more peace-smart, perhaps they can give their permission to have the stories published in the school newspaper.

**2** **Organize a peace auction.**
Raise money to promote peace at your school. With the help of staff, collect donations from parents, community service organizations, and local businesses.

Money from the auction could be used to:

*   send students to camp who would like to but don't have the money to do it. It costs about $150 per week for one student. There are camps where teens can learn leadership skills and hone their communication and problem-solving abilities. The kids who go to summer camps could be in charge of promoting peace in the next school year.

*   establish a teen center at your school for evening activities such as games, dances, study groups, and workshops.

*   create more after-school programs for kids who need a place to go after school.

*   help single parents with odd-jobs around the house, with providing cooked meals for them once a week, or baby-sitting services.

# Peace Projects
## For School

**3** **Conduct a Peace-Smart summit.**
Organize a group of students who would like to reach out into the community to gather all interested people to come together in the name of peace. This could be done on a day before summer break or right before a long school holiday, so that students can use the summit to think about peace as an alternative when they will find themselves with time on their hands. Invite the entire student body, parents, and the community. But remember, it doesn't matter how many people turn out, what matters is that you are giving an important message by organizing this event. Ideas could include:

* inviting senior citizens to share their wisdom during a panel discussion.

* inviting victims of violence to share their personal experiences and how they are coping personally with the tragic consequences of violence.

* asking police officers and youth advocates to conduct workshops on violence intervention.

* asking students to hold panel discussions about what they are doing at home and at school to become more peace-smart.

**4** **Create your own school safety program.**
Review your school's policy for keeping students safe. In your mind is it adequate? Are there things that the school officials should know about that you know about? Should the students be asked questions regarding school safety? You could start out by giving a Student Survey to find out if students at your school feel safe, and if not, what they would like to see done about it. Work with school staff, then, to compile the answers you find on the survey, discuss them, and decide which ones might be needed at your school. Then write (or rewrite) a school safety program which has the input and backing of the student body.

# **Peace Projects**
## For School

**5** Create a special "peace place" in your classroom or school.
Is there a place where kids can sit and relax to think? or to read about peace-smart people? or to discuss peace-smart ideas? Designate a place and make it special by:

* putting posters up which inspire peace

* inviting student and adult volunteers to be there to encourage kids to come in and enjoy peace

* asking peace-smart people in your neighborhood to hold discussions there

* using the space to promote peace at your school in whatever ways the students would like to!

**6** Help authorities with truancy problems.
One of the factors related to juvenile crime is missing school. How does your school handle truancy problems? Read the proactive suggestions below and decide which would be appropriate actions for your school. Present your ideas to the administration and discuss how you can begin to take positive steps to eradicate truancy at your school.

* Parents must call an "absent hotline" and report the reason their child won't be in school that day. Those parents of children who are absent without permission, get a call from the principal, a vice-principal, or a teacher at the school that evening to find out what is going on.

* Train adult volunteers to visit homes who have children that are regularly truant. Maybe parents don't know what is going on and need to be informed.

* Conduct school-wide assemblies on a regular basis to give students information about the advantages of a high school diploma. For instance, police officers could give statistics about reduced chances of dying from a violent crime; other authorities could site the financial advantages of education; sports authorities or other people youth admire could share personal stories of what their education meant to them and how it has helped them succeed in life.

* Form peer groups who support students at risk of failing school. Give help with homework and encouragement to keep coming to school.

* Offer after school programs which youth would want to attend. Provide sports opportunities, career guidance; mentors; peace-smart activities; and fun service learning experiences to broaden horizons and give hope for the future.

# Chapter 5

# Keeping Relationships
# PEACE-SMART

In 1992, 78% of murder victims were killed by someone they knew.[1] According to FBI reports, in the U S, a woman is beaten every 9 seconds by an intimate partner.[2] The violence in day-to-day relationships is staggering and teens, no matter what their circumstances or socio-economic status, need information, skills, and resources to deal effectively with a potentially violent relationship.

In this chapter, we begin by giving teens opportunities to access their relationship to adults in authority. Why? Because before most young people will feel comfortable getting the help they may need, they must first develop a trusting relationship to some caring adults with the authority to help them. So often youth are isolated from the adults around them. Through offering ways to examine their assumptions about adults in authority and teaching them the ways adults can help, Peace Smarts gives youth hope to be part of a team working toward a more peaceful future. We then explore other types of relationships, such as sexual partners and friends.

The adult facilitator will find **Peace Tools** in the following three categories:

* Relationships with authority figures, such as police and teachers (Peace Tools # 40-43)

* Dating and relationships with the opposite sex (Peace Tools # 44-47)

* Relationships with friends (Peace Tools # 48-50)

---

1  FBI, "Crimes in the United States," Uniform Crime Reports,
Washington DC: US Department of Justice, 1992, p.13
2  Ibid, p.16

# For Discussion

1. Why do teens rebel against adult authority?

2. What makes it easy to respect adults? What makes it difficult?

3. Who are adults that you respect? Why?

4. Given your ideal world, how would adults such as parents, teachers, and police treat teens? Be specific.

5. What do you think is needed for adults and teens to work well together? Is this even possible? Why or why not?

6. Who are the most significant, influential people in your life? Why?

7. What do you do to make your relationships peace-smart?

8. Do girls understand boys? Why or why not?

9. Do boys understand girls? Why or why not?

10. What is most needed for boys and girls to understand one another better?

11. Who is a good friend of the opposite sex? What makes this person a friend?

12. How does sex change male-female friendships?

13. Did you ever have a problem getting along with someone of the opposite sex? What did you do about it? How did it turn out?

14. What makes the ideal friend?

15. How have you built trust with a friend? Tell what happened.

16. When you have a problem with a friend, what do you usually do about it?

17. Is it easy or difficult for you to say, "No," to a friend? Explain.

18. When a friend has put pressure on you, have you ever reacted violently?

19. Is it easy to take advantage of friends?

20. In what ways have you taken advantage of a friend? In what ways were you taken advantage of?

21. Has a friend ever been physically or verbally abusive to you? What did you do about it?

22. Do you know someone in an abusive friendship? What advice would you give them?

23. What are the character traits a person needs to walk away from an abusive friendship?

24. When a friend is in trouble, how do you usually react?

25. How would you describe a peace-smart friendship?

## Peace Tool # 40

# ADULT AUTHORITY: WHAT ARE OUR ASSUMPTIONS?

**Directions:** How kids respond to adults in authority has a lot to do with the assumptions they make about the adults.

Do we assume the person is "out to get us?" Do we assume the person doesn't want to help us? Assuming means we don't know all the facts and make a hasty judgment as a result. Usually that judgment is incorrect.

**Below are situations which kids sometimes have to deal with.**

* First write what the "problem assumption" might be, that is, what the teen must be assuming that WON'T resolve the conflict.

* Then write a "better assumption" which could lead to the adult and teen respecting one another and understanding one another better. The first one has been done as an example for you.

| Situation | Problem Assumption | Better Assumption |
|---|---|---|
| City police are setting an evening curfew for teens. | Police hate teens. | Police are trying to keep the streets safe for everyone. |
| The principal stands outside after school directing student traffic. | | |
| There are more adults than ever at the teen center dances. | | |
| A single Mom calls her daughter while she is at her friend's house. | | |
| A father refuses to let his son have the family car to travel out of state. | | |
| Several police officers are gathering on a corner where kids usually hang out. | | |
| A teacher is taking a student out of class as you walk by. | | |
| A man gets out of his car and walks over to a group of teens. | | |
| A security guard at school has a boy by the arm, steering him toward the principal's office. | | |
| A group of angry parents are leaving the local teen center. | | |

# POLICE AND YOUTH: PARTNERS FOR A POSITIVE FUTURE

**Directions:** What has to happen for youth and police to work together? to respect one another? to appreciate one another?

## Below are statements about the police.

* Circle A if you agree with the statement; D, if you disagree.
* Then in a small group discuss how you responded to each statement.
* When you are finished, think and talk about the questions below.

A/D  Police are out to get teens.

A/D  Most police abuse their authority.

A/D  The police I know are nice to teens.

A/D  Most kids I know don't like the police.

A/D  The police around here are always meddling in other people's business.

A/D  Police are just trying to do their jobs.

A/D  I don't trust any officer.

A/D  The police get on my nerves.

A/D  I would enjoy working with the police.

A/D  I realize that the police are risking their lives to help others.

A/D  Police think they can boss people around.

A/D  I have meet some real nice police officers.

A/D  I would feel safe going to the police with information.

A/D  The police in my neighborhood understand teens.

A/D  I would like to see the police more visible around my school and community.

## Questions to think about and discuss:

* What is needed for teens and police to work together well?

* What steps are you willing to take to have a better relationship with the local police?

* Who is a police officer that you trust? What are his/her characteristics?

* What can you tell your friends to help them better understand the police?

* If you were a police officer, what would you do to better serve teens?

* What advice would you give to a police officer who works to prevent violence among teens?

* What have you learned today as a result of thinking about your feelings about the police as authority figures?

## Peace Tool # 42

# TEACHERS AND YOUTH: PARTNERS FOR A POSITIVE FUTURE

**Directions:** What has to happen for youth and teachers to work better together? to respect one another? to appreciate one another?

## Below are statements about teachers.

* Circle A if you agree with the statement; D, if you disagree.
* Then in a small group discuss how you responded to each statement.
* When you are finished, think and talk about the questions below.

A/D   All teachers care about is getting the summer off.

A/D   Most teachers I know really care about kids.

A/D   Too many teachers aren't doing their jobs.

A/D   A teacher works many extra hours.

A/D   Teachers are usually dedicated to helping kids.

A/D   I know at least one teacher I can trust.

A/D   Most kids I know go to teachers for help when they have a serious problem.

A/D   When I think about it, a teacher doesn't have an easy life.

A/D   Teachers are overpaid for what they do.

A/D   Teachers don't get enough respect from kids.

A/D   Teachers don't get enough respect from parents.

A/D   There aren't enough teachers who really care.

A/D   A lot of teachers try to tell kids what to do.

A/D   The teachers I know really listen to kids.

A/D   Overall I respect teachers and think they are doing there best.

## Questions to think about and discuss:

1. What is needed for teens and teachers to work together well?

2. What steps are you willing to take to have a better relationship with some teachers that you know?

3. Who is a teacher that you trust? What are his/her characteristics?

4. What can you tell your friends to help them better understand teachers?

5. If you were a teacher, what would you do to better serve teens?

6. What advice would you give to a teacher who works to prevent violence among teens?

7. What have you learned today as a result of thinking about your feelings about teachers as authority figures?

**100**

# TRUSTING AUTHORITY

**Directions:** Do you trust adults in authority? Do you believe in your heart and soul that most adults are there to help you? that they want to help you?

**Becoming peace-smart means learning to trust adults to use their authority well.**

**In the space below each question:**

✳ Write your own response. Don't think about it too long. Write the first thing that comes to your mind.

✳ When you are finished with all the questions, share your answers with an adult you trust. Talk about ways to increase your trust in adult authority and how that trust can lead to a more peaceful lifestyle for you.

**1. Has something happened to you which causes you to distrust adults? If so, explain briefly.**

_____

_____

**2. Who is an adult that you trust? How did you come to trust this person? Was it an easy or difficult thing to do? Explain.**

_____

_____

**3. Who is an adult that you don't trust? Why? Can anything be done to regain trust and confidence in this person? If so, what?**

_____

_____

**4. What adults in authority do you usually trust (such as teachers, doctors, police, etc.)? What adults in authority do you usually distrust? Why do you think this is the case? What can you do to increase your trust in authority figures?**

_____

_____

_____

**5. Give your own definition of trust. How can trusting adults in authority help teens lead more peaceful lives?**

_____

_____

**Peace Tool # 44**

# SEXUAL HARASSMENT: WHAT IS IT?

**Directions:** Below are definitions of "sexual harassment." Read them alone or with a friend.

## Sexual Harassment can be any of the following:

*   Any unwanted sexual advance

*   Sexual jokes or demeaning gender remarks

*   Verbal or physical behavior from someone which interferes with your privacy

*   Words which annoy or alarm you such as sweetie, babe, hot buns, big boobs, good looking stud

*   Tone of voice, body language, gestures of a sexual nature meant to make you feel intimidated

## Sexual harassment can make you feel:

*   angry

*   confused

*   embarrassed

*   alone

*   hopeless

## Sexual harassment can occur:

*   Between people who know each other well

*   Among acquaintances

*   At school, home, or at work or anywhere where people are gathered

*   Explain why the following are incidents of sexual harassment.

*   Write your ideas in the space below each example.

**Peace Tool # 44**

## *Continuation* SEXUAL HARASSMENT: WHAT IS IT?

Amy was in a hurry after school to get to her doctor's appointment. No one was in the hall, but Pete. He came up to her and blocked her way. At first she thought he was just kidding and she tried explaining that she was in a hurry, so would he please move? He just smiled slowly, blocked her way, and started telling her how sexy she was, and what he would like to do to her. She went from being angry to being totally embarrassed. She was still trying to get past him, when a teacher appeared in the hall, and he turned quickly, so she was able to get away. He yelled after her that he wasn't done with her yet.

_____

_____

_____

Nick has been receiving anonymous letters saying how great his body is, how sexy he looks, and what a thrill it was to watch him move. Nick is offended by these letters and would like them to stop. He feels hopeless as to what to do about them.

_____

_____

_____

Sally has recently moved to town and has a part-time job at a fast-food restaurant. Her manager calls her names like sweetie, chick, and babe while he winks at her or moves his tongue over his lips. Sally is really uncomfortable and scared.

_____

_____

_____

* What do these three examples have in common?

* Have you or a friend experienced sexual harassment? If so, what was done about it?

* What did you do to recover?

* Who were the people that assisted you?

**For information about what to do about sexual harassment, go on to Peace Tool # 45.**

## Peace Tool # 45

# SEXUAL HARASSMENT: WHAT TO DO ABOUT IT

**Directions: Use the information below to take action, if you need to!**

If sexual harassment happens to you, you can:

* Using clear language tell the harasser to stop. Remember you have a right to be in environments that feel safe to you.

* Seek help from a trusted friend, parent, teacher, or counselor. Explain the situation and ask them what would be the best course of action to take.

* Treat the situation as serious. Even if the harasser says he/she is only teasing and even if some of your friends say you are being "overly sensitive," what matters most is what you feel. And if you feel uncomfortable in any way and the harasser keeps continuing even though you have made it clear you want the harassment to stop, know that this is a very serious situation.

* Keep a written record. If you write down the time, place, and circumstances of the harassment, that will help in putting an end to it. Also, it can be very useful to authorities to have the names of witnesses, friends, relatives, etc., whom you have told about the harassment while it was going on.

**In the lines below write other things you could do to stop sexual harassment:**

_____

_____

_____

_____

_____

## An action step you can take:

Does your school have a sexual harassment policy?

If you work, does your workplace have one?

Have you read these policies? If you are unfamiliar with them, ask to see a copy and acquaint yourself with them. If no such policies exist, take an important step and meet with the adult staff responsible who can begin to create a policy.

# 104

# BOYS & GIRLS TALKING TOGETHER

## Directions: Think about these questions:

* Does it seem like a struggle to communicate effectively with the opposite sex?

* Do you try to express yourself, but end up feeling bewildered, perplexed, angry? Do you find yourself impatient much of the time, even though the other person is very special to you?

To communicate better with the opposite sex, it can help to examine how society says boys and girls "are supposed to act."

## Step 1

In a small group of "girls only" or "boys only" brainstorm the expectations and roles that are put on us because of our sex. For instance, boys are taught not to cry, show emotion, and to be aggressive; while girls are told to act like a lady, and dress sexy to catch a man. As your group brainstorms their list, someone in the group write what is being said on a large piece of paper.

## Step 2

After you have finished brainstorming, discuss how you feel personally about these cultural roles and expectations. Share any personal experiences you feel comfortable in sharing.

## Peace Tool # 46

# BOYS & GIRLS TALKING TOGETHER *Continuation*

## Step 3

Mix up the groups now to include both boys and girls. Discuss your different lists that you brainstormed and how these roles and expectations get in the way of communicating with the opposite sex. Include in your discussion, some of the following questions:

* What are some of the differences between men and women that you appreciate? Why?

* What are some of the things men and women have in common that can help them respect and understand one another?

* How does having friends of the same sex better help you to communicate with the opposite sex?

* What would you like for boys to understand about girls?

* What would you like for girls to understand about boys?

* What have you learned today about the opposite sex?

* Do you have more compassion for those whom you don't understand? Why or why not?

* What are some things you can do in your everyday life that will help you communicate better with the opposite sex?

**On the lines below, write three things you will begin today!**

1. _____

2. _____

3. _____

# 106

# STOPPING VIOLENCE IN AN INTIMATE RELATIONSHIP

## Directions: Use the information below to take action, if needed!

According to FBI reports, in the United States a woman is beaten every 9 seconds by an intimate partner. Those who monitor rape crisis hot lines have revealed that up to 80 percent of their calls are from women who have been victimized by someone they know.

Many people in such relationships are afraid to get out of the relationship or to assert themselves so they will be treated better. Are you in a violent relationship?

## Does you intimate partner...

* become jealous easily and for no reason?
* control important things in your life such as your friends, finances, where you can go, etc.?
* pressure you to make commitments in the relationship you feel you are not ready to make?
* do things that make you think he/she is trying to isolate you from your support system, such as family or friends?
* want you to meet his/her needs at the drop of a hat?
* blame you for his/her problems or when something goes wrong?
* try to make you feel guilty by saying such things as, "You're hurting me by not doing what I want."
* ever kick, throw, or hurt the family pet?
* force sex when you are tired, ill, or not in the mood?
* say things that are intended to be cruel and hurtful?
* adhere to rigid sex roles, such as seeing women as subservient or inferior to men?
* seem to have a dual personality with big mood swings between nice and cruel?
* have a history of being physically violent?
* break or strike objects to scare you?
* use physical force like shoving, pushing during an argument?

If you recognize your intimate partner in the description above, it is very important to get help immediately. Without help, this pattern of battering will only get worse over time. Take the first step and do one of actions below:

## 1. Talk with a trusted adult.

## 2. Call a local women's or men's center.

## 3. Confide in a trusted teacher or school counselor.

The pattern of violence can be changed. You can be in a peace-smart relationship, but only if you take the first step NOW.

Note: Statistics above taken from: Robin Warshaw, *I Never Called It Rape: The MS Report on Recognizing, Fighting, and Surviving Date and Acquaintance Rape,* Harper and Row, 1988, p. 15.

# REVENGE: WHAT'S SWEET ABOUT IT?

**Directions: Think About This:**

A Senator approached Abraham Lincoln and said, "Mr. President, I believe that enemies should be destroyed." President Lincoln replied, "I agree with you sir, and the best way to destroy an enemy is to make him a friend."

**With a partner or in a small group discuss the following questions below:**

1.   Have you ever had an enemy that turned into a friend? How did it happen?

2.   Didn't Lincoln basically disagree with the senator? Why didn't he say so?

3.   How do you think the senator responded to Lincoln's reply? What did he say?

4.   What must be given up to make an enemy a friend?

5.   How does revenge get in the way of turning an enemy into a friend?

6.   Have you ever sought revenge? What happened? How did you feel afterward? Did the person become a friend or remain an enemy?

7.   What does making an enemy a friend destroy in each of the people involved?

8.   What is sweet about revenge?

9.   Why didn't Lincoln want to revenge his enemies? Why not keep enemies?

10.  What's the value in keeping enemies? Does it make a person feel more powerful to have people to dislike and distrust?

Now consider ways a kid can keep from wanting or seeking revenge when harmed. Go through the list and check the box if it is something you think would work for you.

❑   Tell myself I'll probably get into trouble if I do something rash.

❑   Talk to the person who did this to me with no one else present.

❑   Force myself to think from my head and not from my anger.

❑   Talk to the person who did this to me with an adult or peer mediator present.

❑   Talk to a friend before I do anything.

❑   Forget about it and move on.

❑   Talk with an adult I trust before I do anything.

❑   Think about what I will get out of revenge, if I get it.

❑   Take out my anger in ways that won't hurt me or the other person such as doing strenuous physical exercise.

**(Note: The quotation above was taken from, Duane Sweeney, ed., The Peace Catalog, Press for Peace, 1984, p. 261.)**

# WHAT'S YOUR "CONFLICT STYLE"?

**Directions:** Becoming peace-smart means understanding yourself and how you prefer to resolve conflicts. Different personality types have different ways of dealing with conflict.

## Below is a description of the basic ways.

* Read each description.

* Then continue.

## The Avoider:

This person likes to avoid conflict or even denies that there is one. He or she doesn't like fights, harsh words, or anything that will break the harmony between friends. Avoiders often feel physical symptoms like headaches or stomach problems because they would rather stuff their feelings rather than confront the other person.

## The Confronter:

This person is just the opposite of the avoider. He or she is "in your face" usually with anger. Confronters can let their emotions get the better of them and react with physical violence or verbal abuse. They are loud, aggressive, and can be judgmental. Usually, though, confronters are "more bark than bite" when the other person remains calm and committed to a working out a solution. Two confronters confronting one another when they are angry, however, can mean trouble.

## The Accommodater:

This person will compromise fast and not spend much time arguing. He or she recognizes that there is a problem, usually thinks the problem is his or her own fault, and will seek to give in. Apologetic and indecisive, accommodaters don't like fighting and usually will change their opinion to keep the peace.

## The Negotiator:

This person will try to work out the conflict without denial, force, or too much compromise. He or she will hold on to their own ideas, while working hard to listen to the other person's side of it, too. Negotiators can control their tempers and provide a quiet confidence in the midst of heated moments. When at least one person is a negotiator, the conflict is usually resolved peacefully.

## Peace Tool # 49

# WHAT'S YOUR "CONFLICT STYLE"? *Continuation*

Read each example of a conflict and check which way you would most likely handle the situation if you were in it. Think about the way you *would* respond, not the way you wish you would respond.

## Conflict

| Conflict | Confront with anger | Avoide person or problem | Give in or apologize | Talk until resolved |
|---|---|---|---|---|
| Some kid just pushed your girl (boy) friend | | | | |
| Your best friend lost your new CD and you are mad | | | | |
| You have found out who has been spreading unkind rumors about you | | | | |
| Someone in your class accuses you of cheating on a test in front of the teacher | | | | |
| Your friend has moved away, promised to write, but hasn't after two months | | | | |
| A new kid at school makes fun of you every time you pass him in the hall | | | | |
| Your best friend wants you to skip the last day of school with her, but you need to be there to talk with a teacher about a summer job you really want | | | | |
| At a party, your friend calls you names for not trying pot | | | | |
| You and your friend are watching football on TV and start arguing over which is the better team | | | | |
| At a school dance, your friend from another school shows up even though she knows she's not supposed to be there | | | | |
| A key player on your basketball team refuses to throw the ball to you during games, so you aren't getting that many chances to score | | | | |
| A friend believes lies about you rather than the truth | | | | |
| A girl at school is always bragging about her rich father and making fun of your father | | | | |
| This is the third time your friend has been late and you are sick and tired of always waiting for him | | | | |
| Your best friend is in trouble and won't tell you the whole story; you feel left out | | | | |

## Reflection:

* Did you observe a pattern? Do you usually solve conflicts in one or two ways?
* Did you use all four ways for solving conflicts throughout?
* Did you notice that your choice for resolving the conflict depended upon the type of conflict?
* If you know someone well, do you usually talk through your problems with them?
* When something happens fast, like someone pushing you or a friend, do you usually resort to confrontation?

**Peace Tool # 50**

# USING DIFFERENT CONFLICT STYLES

**Directions: Do this activity when you have completed Peace tool #49.**

**First:** Form a Small Group

Get together with three others to form a small group of **four**.

Cut out the eight cards below and put them in some sort of container in the middle of the group. Notice that the cards have key words on them which explain the four conflict styles. Each style is repeated twice to give players a chance to role play two people with the same style.

**Second:** Role Play Several Different Conflicts

Choose conflicts listed in **Peace Tool** #49 to role play.

For every conflict role play, two people each select a card. They role play the situation using the conflict style each one has selected.

The other two people observe the role play, watch what is happening, and if appropriate, offer advice.

**Third:** Think About the Consequences of Different Conflict Styles

**While actually role playing:**

* How does it feel like to be in that particular style?

* What's comfortable about it? What's uncomfortable?

* After several role plays, do you notice a pattern emerging with each style? For instance, when in the confronter role, do conflicts often escalate? When in the accommodater one, do the conflicts get over quickly? Does negotiation take more time and patience?

* Which styles have easier consequences to live with?

* Which styles are more effective for resolving conflicts?

**While watching the role play:**

* What would you be doing differently in this situation?

* What are you learning about communication in the four different styles?

* Is there any way you can intervene or offer advice to the pair having the conflict?

* Which style/s most suit you? Why?

# USING DIFFERENT CONFLICT STYLES *Continuation*

## Avoider: Avoids Conflict

## Avoider: Avoids Conflict

## Confronter: Confronts with Anger

## Confronter: Confronts with Anger

## Accommodater: Compromises Fast

## Accommodater: Compromises Fast

## Negotiator: Talks to Resolution

## Negotiator: Talks to Resolution

# Peace Projects

**1** **Develop a Peace Savings Account.**
You can do this alone or with friends. Each day write one or two things that you did that was peace-smart that day. Stayed calm when my friend yelled at me; did my chores without complaining; or helped my friend deal with his Dad, are examples of what you could write down. You could write in a special notebook or blank book, if you like. The purpose is to keep track of peace-smart moves and before you know it, you will have a long list. Just do two a day and watch how fast your list grows. Before you know it, you will have a savings account of **Peace-Smart** ideas! You can then read over your long list with a friend when you both need inspiration for living peace-smart!

**2** **Design a performance about dating violence.**
Gather creative friends together to design a skit, play, or dance performance showing the problems associated with dating violence and what teens can do about them. Spend time researching the topic; use ideas from personal interviews, so you can include real-life experiences in your performance, too. Make arrangements to perform your pieces at a teen center, school, or community playhouse. Invite adults who work with teens on these issues to speak after some of the performances.

**3** **Organize Party Peace Patrols.**
Friends like to get together to party. This can be fun. It doesn't have to be dangerous. Teen Party Patrols work with parents and police to make sure that no weapons, drugs, or any other hazard show up at private parties in the neighborhood. How to get started? Here are a few ideas:

* The Teen Patrol would get the word out to kids who have unchaperoned parties that your group is working with the police to eliminate weapons, drugs, and alcohol at all teen parties in the neighborhood. You could write a letter and get the police and/or other prominent adults in your community to sign it, too!

* Ask your school to distribute copies of the letter to all parents.

* Make a directory available about the hazards of guns, drugs, and alcohol at teen parties. Invite local businesses to advertise in the directory to help cover your expenses. Hand out the directory to all parents. You could also work with police and put down the legal problems parents will have if someone is hurt at their house as a result of an illegal substance or action.

Take special actions at special times such as holidays or graduations. During times when lots of kids will want to party, the Teen Party Patrol can conduct an awareness campaign at schools, teen centers, and community centers, such as libraries.

# Chapter 6

# PEACE SMART
# Neighborhoods

Community involvement is not merely a way for youth to feel good about themselves, but it also is an integral way of helping to solve social problems. More and more we adults are seeing the value of teens' service learning activities. An estimated 30-40% of schools across the country are now trying various ways to attract, cajole, or prod young people into community service.[1] Yet, sometimes what starts out as a requirement turns out to be a heart-opening experience that many youth continue on their own.

In a seminal research study of people who were superior change agents in their communities it was found that the single most important pattern in their lives was "a constructive, enlarging engagement" with other people.[2] In other words, adults who contributed significantly to their communities were those who understood early in their lives that they belonged to a larger group, outside of the family, and grew to appreciate their role in influencing that group. As they contributed to others, their spheres of influence gradually expanded to include more and more people. As the authors of the study pointed out, "Our prosperity as social beings is woven by patterns of kinship, mutual assistance, and affection."[3]

In this chapter adults can help teens find ways to expand their spheres of influence outside of home and school. In so doing youth experience grassroots involvement and leadership in their neighborhoods for addressing issues of violence that matter to them. Taking the skills learned in the previous chapters, teens are now ready to implement them in community settings. Beginning with looking at how assumptions about individuals affect the common good, teens then think about, plan, and take action for making a difference in their communities.

**The Peace Tools in this chapter are designed specifically for:**

\*    Developing skills for promoting peace with others in the community (Peace Tools # 51-58)

---

1   "Youth Volunteers," in The Los Angeles Times, August 24 1997, p. A12

2   Laurent Parks Daloz, et Al, Common Fire: Lives of Committment in a Complex World, Beacon Press, 1996, p. 63

3   Ibid, p. 64

# For Discussion

1.  Have you ever been a victim of prejudice? Explain.

2.  What assumptions about others could lead to prejudice?

3.  How would you rate your neighborhood? Racist or not? What are the root causes of racism?

4.  In your ideal world, how would people with different views resolve their conflicts?

5.  How close does your own neighborhood come to this ideal? What can you do to bring it closer to your ideal?

6.  Do you feel safe in your neighborhood? Why or why not?

7.  If you were a member of your local police, what would you do to make your neighborhood safer?

8.  Why do you think kids join gangs? Have you ever known a gang member? What did you do?

9.  How can kids be enticed away from gangs or gang-like behavior?

10. What would you advise adults to do about the problems of gangs in a neighborhood?

11. Do you think your community has adequate resources for helping victims of violence, such as enough shelters for abused women, adequate places for teens to go to get away from abusive parents? If not, how can more be developed? What could you do to help this situation?

12. What does it mean to advocate for peace in your neighborhood? How could you go about doing that?

13. What does it mean to enlarge your "circle of influence?" Who are the people you influence on a daily basis?

14. List the attributes of someone who is committed to the common good.

15. Do you know someone in your community who is known for helping others? What do you admire most about this person?

16. Have you been helped by this person or by someone like him or her? Explain.

17. In your opinion what would it take to get more youth involved with promoting peace and non-violent problem-solving in their neighborhoods?

18. How would you like the adults in your community to communicate with you? talk to you? view you? relate to you? And what can you do to improve your relationships with these adults?

19. What could you do today to mend any fences between adults and youth in your community?

20. Do you think most teens are open to working with the adults in their communities? Why or why not?

21. What assumptions and expectations get in the way of teens and adults working well together in your neighborhood?

22. What organizations exist in your community to empower teens?

23. Is there something you want to say or do in your community and you don't know how?

24. What mentors, organizations, teachers, parents, or friends can help you make this happen?

25. Imagine your neighborhood five years from now. What has changed as a result of promoting peace-smart attitudes and actions?

# PLAY THE ASSUMPTION GAME

**Directions:** Do the assumptions we make help or hinder us in being peace-smart about our neighbors? Play this game and see what happens...

**Number of Players:** 2

**Purpose:** One player make assumptions based on outward appearances. The other player refutes those assumptions, pretending to know the person being talked about. Players take turns until all the character cards are used.

**How to Play:**

1.  Cut out the character cards on the next page and place them face down in front of you.

2.  Player #1 picks one of the cards.

3.  From the perspective of this person, Player #1 makes an assumption about one of the people listed below.

4.  Player #2 pretends to know the person and refutes the assumption with facts. Player #2 begins by saying, "Your assumption is incorrect. I know this person and the facts are:" Player #2 should strive to make the facts about the person positive to show that the assumption made has treated the person unfairly or that the assumption is way off-base.

5.  Then Player #2 picks a character card and the process is repeated.

6.  Players can make or refute more than one assumption about anyone listed.

7.  When all the character cards have been used, players discuss the questions listed below.

# 116

*Continuation* **PLAY THE ASSUMPTION GAME**

## Character Cards:

| | |
|---|---|
| Old Grandma | Principal of the Local Public School |
| Teen from a Wealthy School | Homeless Man |
| Experienced Local Police Officer | Confident Athlete |
| New Mailman on the Route | Someone New in the Neighborhood |
| Young Mother with a Baby | Father out for a walk with his Son |
| Heavyweight Boxer | Martial Arts Expert |
| University Student | Well–dressed Businessman |
| Troubled Teen | Tired Truck Driver |
| Single Mother of Four Children | Teen Girl in a Hurry |

## Make Assumptions About the Following People in Your Neighborhood or How They May View You:

* a young woman wears a tattered coat to a community meeting

* an old man asks a person on the street for money

* two teens with tattoos and wild hair are running toward you

* a man with glasses is intently reading on the bus

* a glamorous woman asks for directions to a local TV station

* a 10 year-old girl walking down the street is red-eyed and sad

* an African American man is knocking on your door at 10 PM

* an Asian girl is walking down the street in a short dress and high heels

* the town mayor is going into a pornography shop

* an elderly woman is scolding a teen

* your neighbor is tipsy from drinking too much at the Fourth of July celebration

* the woman down the street always wears funny-looking hats

* a teen you have never seen before is walking slowing looking at the houses on your block

## Questions to Discuss:

1. Was it difficult or easy to make assumptions about certain people? Explain.

2. What did you think or feel when your assumption was refuted?

3. How do hasty judgments about people hurts us?

4. What are possible ways to morph the habit of making assumptions and jumping to hasty conclusions about people?

5. How can we change negative assumptions into positive ones?

6. Explain how thinking well of people can lead to more peace-smart neighborhoods.

**Peace Tool # 51**

## *Continuation* PLAY THE ASSUMPTION GAME

**Character Cards:**

| | |
|---|---|
| Old Grandma | Principal of the Local Public School |
| Teen from a Wealthy School | Homeless Man |
| Experienced Local Police Officer | Confident Athlete |
| New Mailman on the Route | Someone New in the Neighborhood |
| Young Mother with a Baby | Father out for a walk with his Son |
| Heavyweight Boxer | Martial Arts Expert |
| University Student | Well-dressed Businessman |
| Troubled Teen | Tired Truck Driver |
| Single Mother of Four Children | Teen Girl in a Hurry |

## Make Assumptions About the Following People in Your Neighborhood or How They May View You:

* a young woman wears a tattered coat to a community meeting

* an old man asks a person on the street for money

* two teens with tattoos and wild hair are running toward you

* a man with glasses is intently reading on the bus

* a glamorous woman asks for directions to a local TV station

* a 10 year-old girl walking down the street is red-eyed and sad

* an African American man is knocking on your door at 10 PM

* an Asian girl is walking down the street in a short dress and high heels

* the town mayor is going into a pornography shop

* an elderly woman is scolding a teen

* your neighbor is tipsy from drinking too much at the Fourth of July celebration

* the woman down the street always wears funny-looking hats

* a teen you have never seen before is walking slowing looking at the houses on your block

## Questions to Discuss:

1. Was it difficult or easy to make assumptions about certain people? Explain.

2. What did you think or feel when your assumption was refuted?

3. How do hasty judgments about people hurts us?

4. What are possible ways to morph the habit of making assumptions and jumping to hasty conclusions about people?

5. How can we change negative assumptions into positive ones?

6. Explain how thinking well of people can lead to more peace-smart neighborhoods.

## Peace Tool # 52

# YOUR PLACE IN YOUR NEIGHBORHOOD

**Directions:** Where are the needs in your neighborhood? To be a peace-advocate, you first need to know "Who needs help?"

In the spaces below, alone or with a friend:

* Brainstorm ideas about the types of actions you can take in the places indicated.

* For instance, in the elementary school, you might write in, "Volunteer to help a child." This in itself is a peace-smart move because children who do well in school are less likely to get into trouble with the law.

* Or in the church, you might write, "Find out about gangs."

* Think about the places in your neighborhood that could use your help in working for peace. Think about what you would like to do to help your neighborhood become more peace-smart.

# DE-GLAMORIZE GANGS AND GUNS

**Directions: Take a stand against gangs and guns in your neighborhood.**

* Read each section below and discuss your ideas with a friend or a caring adult. Then:
**TAKE ACTION**, if needed.

### Section I: **Gangs**

Read each statement below and tell what you think about each one.

1. Gangs are groups of people who identify themselves with each other through the use of a common name, common area or territory, common rivals or enemies, exclusive membership and most importantly, acting with antisocial behavior associated with crime.

2. Violence is inherent in gang activity. Street gang members climb the ladder of respect by committing criminal acts.

3. Often such criminal acts are at the expense of innocent and uninvolved people.

4. Gang members believe violence will be rewarded within their group and will use this belief to rationalize their actions.

## Do you know anyone who shows any of these red flags of gang involvement?

* Practices gang signs (hand signs) at home in the mirror or at school

* Uses street slang to disguise true meanings of words

* Has several older acquaintances

* Shows aggressive behavior toward adults in authority

* Drops in school attendance, grades, or doesn't see the relevancy of school anymore

* Has increase curiosity in weapons or knows a great deal about weapons

* Has unexplained injuries

* Away from home or school for long periods of time with no explanations

* Flirts with "gangster" dress code

If you are concerned about a family member or a friend, tell an adult you trust. Also, if your school or teen organization would like a gang awareness program, contact your local police for more information. By working with the officers in your community, together you can both get much more accomplished than either of you can do alone!

# DE-GLAMORIZE GANGS AND GUNS *Continuation*

### Section 2: **Guns**

Did you know that on July 24, 1996, Senators Bill Bradley, Arlen Specter, and Paul Wellstone passed a Senate Resolution designating Oct., 10, 1996 as the "Day of National Concern About Young People and Young Violence?" On that day, millions of students from around the country were asked to sign a pledge. This "Pledge Against Gun Violence," renounced careless gun use and affirmed the power your choices have in making your community peace-smart.

Below is a copy of that Pledge. (Made available from Mothers Against Violence in America, Seattle, WA) Copy it and make it available to all your friends to sign. How many pledges can you and others gather? Make people in your neighborhood aware of these pledges by one or more of these actions:

* Displaying them at the local public library

* Showing them to elementary students and having them make the pledge, too

* Pasting them over gang graffiti

* Making a large mural out of them for public display in your town center or mall

* Presenting them to the mayor and City Council for their comment, advice, and explanation on what they are doing to help make your community peace-smart

---

## *Pledge Against Gun Violence*

I will *never* bring a gun to school.

I will *never* use a gun to settle a dispute.

I will use my influence with my friends
to keep them from using guns to settle disputes.

My individual choices and actions, when multiplied by those of young people throughout the country, will make a difference. Together, by honoring this pledge, we can reverse the violence and grow up in safety.

**Signature** _____     **Date** _____

---

# 120

# ADVOCATE TO END DOMESTIC VIOLENCE

## Directions:

* Take the test below and discuss your answers with a friend.

* Compare your answers to the correct answers (at the bottom of the page).

* Then write down your ideas on the lines under the questions.

## Test Your Knowledge of Domestic Violence

1. What is the greatest risk factor of being a victim of domestic violence?
   a. Poverty   b. Race   c. Income   d. Gender

2. Every_____ seconds a woman in the U.S. is beaten by her partner.
   a. 9   b. 15   c. 30   d. 60

3. When is a battered woman in the most danger of being killed?
   a. When batterer is drinking
   b. If she fights back
   c. When attempting to leave the relationship

4. What percentage of emergency department patients are battered women?
   a. 5-10%   b. 15-20%   c. 30-35%

5. Which facilities are the most abundant in most communities?
   a. Homeless shelters
   b. Women's shelters
   c. Animal shelters

6. What do victims of domestic violence need most?
   a. A safe place to go to escape the abuse
   b. Someone who listens, believes, and does not blame her
   c. A community that does not tolerate domestic violence
   d. All of the above

**Written by Valerie Strafford, Director, Citizens Against Domestic Violence, Oak Harbor, WA**

**Used with permission**

**Quiz answers:**
1. d; 2. a; 3. c; 4. c; 5. c; 6. d

## Peace Tool # 54

# ADVOCATE TO END DOMESTIC VIOLENCE *Continuation*

Have you ever been a victim of domestic violence?     YES     NO

Has a friend or family member ever been a victim?     YES     NO

In the last six months, have you read a book or article about domestic violence?   YES     NO

What is it about domestic violence that you find most difficult to understand?

_____

_____

_____

What can your community do to help victims of domestic violence?

_____

_____

_____

What organizations would help fund a shelter for abused women?
What can you do to convince them this is a worthwhile project?

_____

_____

_____

What actions can you and other teens make to help end domestic violence in your community?

_____

_____

_____

# 122

## REVISIONING THE AMERICAN DREAM

### Directions:

* Read the following story with a friend or family member.

* Then discuss the questions below.

**(This story is taken from the book, Teenage Violence, by Elaine Landau.**
**Check it out from your local library for a detailed look at this problem written especially for teens.)**

"It was supposed to have been the American dream. Yusuf K. Hawkins, a black sixteen-year-old honor student, was about to purchase his first car. He had seen an ad for a used Pontiac in a weekly shopper's guide. Maybe now it was Yusuf's turn to enjoy a piece of the dream—to acquire a possession often considered symbolic of emergence into manhood. To many young men, a car is more than just a mode of transportation; it's often associated with freedom, independence, and adulthood.

Therefore, it's not surprising that the teenager sounded excited when he called to find out more about the vehicle. Hawkins also sounded knowledgeable as he inquired about the car's mileage and engine problems. He asked for directions to Bensonhurst, the predominantly white section of Brooklyn, New York, where the car's owner resided.

The person at the other end of the phone was Nick Hadzinas, a twenty-five-year old construction worker who had come to America from Salonika, Greece, just over two years earlier. Hadzinas left his homeland to find a better life inn America or, as a friend described it, "because he planned on living the American dream."

It was arranged that Hawkins would stop by that evening to inspect the car...But that's not what happened. Following Hadzinass' directions, he took a subway train to Bensonhurst. He was accompanied by three of his friends...the boys arrived in Bensonhurst...and were jumped by a gang of about ten angry white youths...Someone in the mob shouted, "Let's club the niggers..."Within moments the violence escalated. According to witnesses, one of the whites took out a gun. As he aimed it at Hawkins and pulled the trigger, he yelled, "The hell with beating them up." Four shots rang out...Yusuf Hawkins may have hoped to drive out of Bensonhurst that night in his own car, but instead he was carried out as a corpse. The hopes, dreams, and life of a sixteen-year-old honor student were extinguished by a bullet from the gun of a boy he'd never seen before.

The American dream had clouded as well for Nick Hadzinas, who had only wanted to sell his car, not ignite a violent incident that resulted in a brutal killing. After Hawkins's death, Hadzinas took the car off the market.

**Peace Tool # 55**                                    123

# REVISIONING THE AMERICAN DREAM *Continuation*

1. How did violence interrupt the dreams of the two boys in this story?

_____

_____

2. Do you know someone whose dream was cancelled because of violence? What happened?

_____

_____

3. What would you have done if you were Nick? Would you have taken the car off the market, too? Would you have been depressed about the incident? Why or why not?

_____

_____

4. How can we re-vision this story? What could have happened if the violence were not present?

_____

_____

5. On the lines below, write your ideas about the American Dream. How can we have a future without violence? What things teens can do to help make the America Dream possible for more people? To help eradicate violence in our communities?

_____

_____

_____

_____

_____

_____

_____

_____

_____

_____

_____

_____

## 124

# HOW TO CHOOSE PEACE

**Directions:** To help others, it's important that you stay on track. Sometimes this is not so easy. When a friend is teasing you and you can feel your anger rising; when someone at a school dance continues to push and shove you; when some wise kids in the back of the class keeps making jokes about you.

## How can you stay cool and model living from a peace-smarts ethic?

* One very good way is to develop an inner resource state so you can stay calm when you feel yourself slipping.

* You can also tell your friends about it, explain why you use it, and suggest they try it, too.

## Here's how it works:

### First,

Think of a time when something happened and you really felt great—really wonderful. Maybe it was a time when...

* at last you got the gift you've been waiting for

* you got an unexpected good grade on a test

* that special person asked you on a date

* you felt really loved and appreciated

Whatever the experience, imagine it now vividly in your head. Go through every detail as if it were happening now. How did you feel? Think about how you felt about yourself, others, and life in general. Pretty good, right?

### OK, next,

write down on a 3X5 card the main ways you feel when you recall this special event. Write down as many good feelings as you can think of. Be as descriptive as possible. Some possibilities might be:

* confident
* happy
* in control of my life
* reassured
* affirmed
* encouraged

# HOW TO CHOOSE PEACE *Continuation*

**Now**

imagine yourself stepping into a warm pool of gorgeous, aqua water. The warm water bathes you in refreshment and contentment. Read all those good feelings you have written on your 3x5 card. In your imagination immerse yourself in the comforting water. Breathe deeply and slowly. Savor all those wonderful feelings. Feel them deeply within yourself as you let the warm water soothe and calm you. This is your **Inner Resource State.** Stay in it as long as you want.

## When you step out of the pool, remember...

∗    you can go back to it anytime you want

∗    when you are in the midst of a problem that bugs you and makes you mad, you can think of your **Resource State** to help calm you and keep you focused on peaceful ways to solve the problem

∗    whenever you want to remind yourself of how wonderful you are, you can think those wonderful thoughts and feel those great feelings that your **Resource State** provides.

## Practice Using Your Inner Resource State:

With a friend, role-play a difficult conversation in which the friend is trying to make you mad. Picture your **Resource State** as he or she is talking to you. Does imagining this help you? Is it easier to stay calm now? Remember to breathe deeply as you are being bugged. Counter the abusive conversation with rational ideas or by walking away. How does your calm demeanor affect your friend?

**Reverse roles** and now <u>you</u> try to make your friend angry, while he or she maintains an inner **Resource State.**

**After your role play**, discuss these questions with your friend:

∗    Is it any fun to bug someone who doesn't get mad easily? Why or why not?

∗    What was easy about staying in your **Resource State**? What was difficult about it?

∗    How does it feel not to get hooked into becoming angry and violent?

∗    What does staying peace-smart mean to you? What could it mean for your friends? the people in your neighborhood?

Practice using your Inner Resource State in everyday life and observe how it works for you.

# 126

# PROMOTING PEACE IN YOUR NEIGHBORHOOD

## Directions: Think about these questions:

* How does a person promote peace?

* What are the skills needed?

* What's the desire and motivation?

* What experiences and personality traits would help?

## Below are more questions.

* Interview someone (or a few people) in your neighborhood by asking them the questions.

* Compare their responses with your own ideas. (If you would like to video or audio tape your interview, you can play it back or let others watch or listen to it!)

1. Give your name, age, and occupation.

2. How would you promote peace in our neighborhood?

3. Do you consider committed to our community? Why or why not?

4. Do you know anyone who is? If so, what do they do?

5. Do you think our community has enough volunteers?

6. How can our community help teens more?

7. If more teens were peace-smart, what would they be doing?

8. How can teens get more involved in their neighborhoods?

9. Have you ever been personally affected by violence?

10. If so, how did this experience change you?

11. What advice would you give teens today wanting to do more for peace?

## When you are finished with your interviews, reflect on:

What have you learned about becoming a peace advocate from this experience? Write your ideas in the space below:

_____

_____

_____

_____

# DEVELOP A CODE FOR CARING

## Part I

**Directions:** The story below gives much to think about regarding the power of caring and resolving conflicts peacefully.

✳    Read it (or have someone read it to you).

✳    Then discuss the questions in a small group.

✳    After you have had a chance to voice your opinions and to hear the opinions of others, move on **Part II.**

### This story is taken from the book, *How Can I Help?*, by Ram Dass

What Can It Teach About Caring?

The train clanked and rattled through the suburbs of Tokyo on a drowsy afternoon. Our car was comparatively empty—a few housewives with their kids in tow, some old folks going shopping. I gazed absently at the drab houses and dusty hedge groves.

At one station the doors opened, and suddenly the afternoon quiet was shattered by a man bellowing violent, incomprehensible curses. The man staggered into our car. He wore laborer's clothing, and he was big, drunk, and dirty. Screaming, he swung at a woman holding a baby. The blow sent her spinning into the laps of an elderly couple. It was a miracle that the baby was unharmed.

Terrified, the couple jumped up and scrambled toward the other end of the car. The laborer aimed a kick at the retreating back of the old woman but missed as she scuttled to safety. This so enraged the drunk that he grabbed the metal pole in the center of the car and tried to wrench it out of its stanchion. I could see that one of his hands was cut and bleeding. The train lurched ahead, the passengers frozen with fear. I stood up.

I was young then, some twenty years ago, and in pretty good shape. I'd been putting in a solid eight hours of Aikido training nearly every day for the past three years. I liked to throw and grapple. I thought I was tough. The trouble was,, my martial skill was untested in combat. As students of Aikido, we were not allowed to fight.

"Aikido," my teacher had said again and again, "is the art of reconciliation. Whoever has the mind to fight has broken his connection with the universe. If you try

**Peace Tool # 58**

## *Continuation* DEVELOP A CODE FOR CARING

to dominate people, you are already defeated. We study how to resolve conflict, not how to start it."

I listened to his words. I tried hard...I felt both tough and holy. In my heart, however, I wanted an absolutely legitimate opportunity whereby I might save the innocent by destroying the guilty.

"This is it!" I said to myself as I got to my feet. "People are in danger. If I don't do something fast, somebody will probably get hurt."

Seeing me stand up, the drunk recognized a chance to focus his rage. "Aha!" he roared. "A foreigner! You need a lesson in Japanese manners."

I held on lightly to the commuter strap overhead and gave him a slow look of disgust and dismissal. I planned to take the turkey apart, but <u>he</u> had to make the first move. I wanted him mad, so I pursed my lips and blew him an innocent kiss.

"All right!" he hollered. "You're gonna get a lesson." He gathered himself for a rush at me.

A fraction of a second before he could move, someone shouted "Hey!" It was earsplitting. I remember the strangely joyous, lilting quality of it...

I wheeled to my left; the drunk spun to his right. We both stared down at a little, old Japanese man. He must have been well into his seventies,, this tiny gentleman, sitting there immaculate in his kimono. He took no notice of me, but beamed delightedly at the laborer, as though he had a most important, most welcome secret to share.

"C'mere," the old man said in an easy vernacular, beckoning to the drunk. "C'mere and talk with me." He waved his hand lightly.

The big man followed as if on a string. He planted his feet belligerently in front of the old gentleman, and roared above the clacking wheels, "Why the hell should I talk to you?" The drunk now had his back to me. If his elbow moved so much as a millimeter, I'd drop him in his socks.

The old man continued to beam at the laborer. "What'cha been drinkin'?" he asked, his eyes sparkling with interest.

"I been drinkin' sake," the laborer bellowed back, "and it's none of your business!" Flecks of spittle spattered the old man.

"Oh, that's wonderful," the old man said, "absolutely wonderful!" You see, I love sake too. Every night, me and my wife (she's seventy-six, you know), we warm

# DEVELOP A CODE FOR CARING *Continuation*

up a little bottle of sake and take it out into the garden, and we sit on an old wooden bench. We watch the sun go down, and we look to see how our persimmon tree is doing. My great grandfather planted that tree, and we worry about whether it will recover from those ice storms we had last winter...

As he struggled to follow the old man's conversation, the drunk's face began to soften. His fists slowly unclenched. "Yeah," he said. "I love persimmons, too..." His voice trailed off.

"Yes," said the old man, smiling, and I'm sure you have a wonderful wife."

"No," replied the laborer. "My wife died." Very gently, swaying with the motion of the train, the big man began to sob. "I don't got no *wife*, I don't got no *home*, I don't got no *job*. I'm so ashamed of myself." Tears rolled down his cheeks; a spasm of despair rippled through his body.

Now it was my turn. Standing there in my well-scrubbed youthful innocence, my...righteousness, I suddenly felt dirtier than he was.

Then the train arrived at my stop. As the doors opened, I heard the old man cluck sympathetically. "My, my," he said, "that is a difficult predicament, indeed. Sit down here and tell me about it."

As the train pulled away, I sat down on a bench. What I had wanted to do with muscle had been accomplished with kind words. I had just seen Aikido tried in combat. I would have to practice the art with an entirely different spirit. it would be a long time before I could truly speak about the resolution of conflict.

## Questions for Discussion

1. Does your opinion of the drunken man change as the story progresses? If so, why?

2. Have you ever been in a similar situation as the narrator of this story—that is, you wanted to punch somebody to "put him in his place." What happened?

3. The Aikido teacher told his student, "Whoever has the mind to fight has broken his connection with the universe." What does this mean to you?

4. Why is the old man so successful in calming the angry man?

5. In our society, kind words and a listening ear are not always considered powerful. How does this story show their power?

6. What do you think the narrator learned form this incident?

7. What moved you most about this story? What will you remember most about it?

# 130

## *Continuation* DEVELOP A CODE FOR CARING

## Part II

**Directions:** Create your own special code of caring. This could be also called your personal ethics about caring.

Fill in the sentences below with ways you would like to become more peace-smart toward others.

**I understand that listening and kind words are more powerful than physical force to resolve conflicts because**

_____

_____

_____

**I want be more caring toward people in my neighborhood by**

_____

_____

_____

**I think it's important for people in my neighborhood to realize that**

_____

_____

_____

**I could promote caring in my community by**

_____

_____

_____

**Violence in my neighborhood could end if only more people**

_____

_____

_____

**I am showing my commitment to promote caring and compassion in my neighborhood by**

_____

_____

_____

Ross/DeGaetano

# Peace Projects
## Neighborhood Peace Projects

**1** **Think! Creative Social Service.**
Partner with police or service organizations in your community to work for peace in creative ways. First, do some research. Find out where the needs are. For instance, you may see that there is no where to go after school for many teens. In your research you will find that many crimes are committed by youth from 3:00-5:00 PM. Keeping kids busy and out of trouble during this time should be a priority. Or you may observe that older kids are hanging out at the local elementary school. In your research you would find that many gangs want to recruit younger kids, because they are easily influenced. Monitoring elementary children to and from school is critical to keeping a peace-smart neighborhood. You and some friends could submit a proposal to your local City Council to create a **Youth Link Board** and begin **ACTION** in these or other areas of concern.

**A Youth Link Board:**

* is comprised of about 8-12 youth and 1-3 adults.

* its job is to advocate for teens in your community by making recommendations to the City Council.

* members of the **Youth Link Board** meet with City Council members to discuss concerns and find ways to create positive solutions.

* members of the **Youth Link Board** in one city were responsible for creating a Skateboard Park and a Teen Center where kids could go to hang out, meet, and get involved in activities such as art, drama, music, and video production.

Remember, adults don't always know what youth want and need. Create a **Youth Link Board** so your voice and creative ideas are heard!

For inspiration on approaching social problems creatively, read all or part of Bill McKibben's book, *Hope, Human and Wild* (Little, Brown, 1996). Here are some examples from the book about how one Brazilian city, Curitiba, uses innovative ideas to get things done:

* Like many cities in Brazil, many abandoned children live on the streets. The mayor of Curitiba persuaded business to adopt children and give them meals and a little money for simple chores.

* When teenagers commit petty crimes or harass people, they are hired to help old people and carry their packages.

* To help adults who cannot read, trailers with teachers and books move into the neighborhoods to teach literacy or vocational skills. People pay very little (the

# 132

# **Peace Projects**

## Neighborhood Peace Projects

equivalent of two bus tokens) to come every day to learn. Classes draw up their own lists of rules, such as, "Don't bring your knife." or "No drugs allowed."

If you have an inspiration or an idea you think will work to help your neighborhood become more peace-smart, let the adults know. Advocate on behalf of your ideas. Don't let anyone tell you, "It cannot be done," because with dedication and determination you can accomplish anything.

## **2** Make life easier for your neighbors.

The antidote to violence is, of course, caring. Helping to make life easier and smoother for others reduces their stressful situations, too! Less stress means it is easier to cope with everyday problems non-aggressively, without harm to ourselves or others. How can you make life easier for people in your neighborhood? Get together with friends and decide on an action to take. Then elicit the help of adults in your community—teachers, business people, parents you know who would like to lend a hand to a worthwhile project. Here are some ideas:

∗   Build wheelchair access ramps so everyone can enjoy parks, museums, restaurants

∗   Adopt a street or part of a neighborhood. Help to educate the children in this locale about the importance of safety and crime prevention. You could develop a brochure to distribute in conjunction with the local police or a social service organization. The National Crime Prevention Council has an excellent brochure, entitled, "How can I protect kids from crime and violence?" You could find ways to make this pamphlet available to people in your adopted locale. For more information about this and other informative materials, contact, 801-486-8768.

∗   Clean up gang graffiti and replace it with positive messages about peace in your neighborhood.

∗   Conduct a local campaign for children to turn in toys guns and violent toys and games, including violent video games to show that violent play should not be child's play. Enlist the help of businesses to give children books, magazine subscriptions, or some other educational gift as a way to reinforce this peace-smart decision.

∗   Hold a canned food drive, or conduct a bake sale to help the needy in your neighborhood.

∗   Organize a Teen Brigade to help single parents in your neighborhood. Single parents are under a lot of stress, they sure could use some of the boundless energy of teens! Can you and some friends...Cook a meal and deliver it to a single parent and his/her

# Peace Projects
## Neighborhood Peace Projects

children? Plan to make a meal for a single-parent household on a regular basis? Can you find restaurants who might donate food and services occasionally? Are there social service agencies you can work with to help baby-sit for single parents?

Develop a Community Resource Directory. List all the places children, teens, and families could get help with problems of violence. Ask local businesses and social service organizations for help with this project.

**3 Develop Youth Think Tanks.**
Big corporations use them. So do science laboratories. The President of the United States has one of his very own. These are **Think Tanks**, where people get together on a regular basis to sit around and think. Yes, people are paid good money to do this. The people in think tanks are usually great problem-solvers and are noted to their innovative approaches to seemingly difficult situations. Would you and some friends like to identify a violence-related problem in your neighborhood and get together to think about it? After all that thinking, though, you will most likely come up with an idea you will want to propose to city officials, the Chamber of Commerce, or some other organization or agency that might want to work with you. Adults in your community may want to join your **Think Tank**. For instance, the Chamber of Commerce would probably agree that it is to their benefit to determine the degree of gang infiltration and how that affects the local business community.

**4 Form a Peer Jury.**
Through the collaboration of schools, police, and the court system this is being done around the country. If your town doesn't have a Peer Jury, you may just want to start one. Here the steps you can take:

* Begin by understanding its role: A Peer Jury is made up of teens who preside over offenses by other teens, such as traffic tickets or burglary. The Peer Jury is authorized to make recommendations as to the type of punishment a crime should have, but the final decision is, of course, with the presiding judge.

* Discuss the idea with a local police officer or teacher. Sometimes police are interested in this because it does help to reduce teen crime. It seems a jury of peers can be very effective in stopping youth crime, especially speeding and drunken driving. Also, social studies teachers at your high school or junior high might be interested as a way to

# Chapter 7

# Practicing
# PEACE SMARTS

"Practice Makes Perfect." Most youth can understand that, whether they have honed their skills on the basketball court or met the challenge of high school graduation. And what is more, teens respect the power inherent in repetition; the self-respect which comes from perfecting a talent or ability through personal effort.

This chapter is designed to provide youth with practice in being peace-smart and to show that the everyday little things are most important when learning and living in peace.

The cumulative experiences throughout childhood and adolescence are what mold character. Those "little things" add up. The challenge for adults in a violent society such as ours is to consistently be available to our children and teens to teach them "peace-smarts." The **Peace Tools** and **Projects** in this chapter provide a needed focus and context for assisting with this challenge. They give youth many opportunities to practice peace-smarts throughout a typical day.

The following **Peace Tools** are divided into three categories:

*   Handling Personal Space and Crowded Spaces—knowing and keeping boundaries (Peace Tools # 59-62)

*   Being Peace-Smart on the Move—using techniques in mobile environments for staying calm and out of trouble (Peace Tools # 63-65)

*   Understanding and Thinking About the Effects of Media Violence (Peace Tools # 66-69)

# For Discussion

1.  What have you practiced a lot and were glad that you did?

2.  Is developing a peaceful attitude and approach to solving problems a skill? Why or why not?

3.  Can people actually learn to be peaceful and get better at it? Why or why not?

4.  What are some ways you could practice being peace-smart in your everyday life?

5.  When someone comes too close to you, what do you usually do?

6.  When someone shoves you while you are in a line? What do you usually do?

7.  Do you think much about maintaining your personal space? Explain.

8.  How do you usually react when you are in a crowded place?

9.  What happens when you encounter an angry driver while you are either in a car or driving yourself?

10. Have you ever encountered any forms of violence while shopping? What did you do?

11. What advice would you give to teens to keep safe when they are traveling from one place to another?

12. How can our society continue to thrive if violence keeps escalating?

13. What can practicing peace smarts by an individual mean for all of society?

14. Do you think your friends would make fun of you if you told them you were practicing peace smarts? Why or why not?

15. What would you do if someone made fun of you?

16. Tell about a time when you let your "angry emotions get the best of you." How did things eventually work out?

17. Tell about a time when you used your head to solve a problem although you were tempted to use physical force. How did things eventually work out?

18. What would you like adults to do to make it easier for you to practice peace smarts?

19. How can you help younger children practice being peace-smart?

20. Finish this sentence: If more people practiced peace smarts...

21. Imagine our society ten years from now. What is happening regarding violence?

22. Imagine your life ten years from now. What do you do to live peacefully and to help others to do so, too?

23. Who do you know whom you can help practice peace smarts?

24. What can you do today to practice peace smarts in your life?

25. What can you do to remind yourself that you are a creative person who can solve problems non-violently?

**Peace Tool # 59**

# KNOW YOUR PERSONAL SPACE

## Directions: Choose a partner and do the activities below.

* Switch roles so that you both have a chance to experience each perspective in each activity.

* When you are finished discuss the questions with your partner or in a small group with others who have done these activities.

### Activity #1

Person A stands still, with eyes closed. Person B starts off about 20 feet away from Person A. Person B starts walking very slowly toward the back of Person A. Person A gets in touch with his/her senses and observes how it feels to have the other person approaching from the back. Person A says, "STOP" when he/she feels Person B getting too close to feel comfortable. Person B stops.

### Activity #2

This is all the same as Activity #1 except now Person B starts walking very slowly toward the front of Person A.

### Activity #3

Person B stands about six feet from Person A. Person A holds out his/her arms in the air, then very slowly brings them down to rest on the side of the body. As Person A is moving his/her arms downward, Person B moves closer and closer to Person A. Person A says, "STOP" when Person B gets too close to feel comfortable. Person B stops.

### Activity #4

A large piece of white butcher paper is put down on the floor. Person A stands in the middle of the paper. Person A predicts how close another person can be and *still feel comfortable* to him or her. Person A indicates this by drawing an O on the paper. Person A also predicts how close another person can be when it starts *to feel uncomfortable* to him or her. Person A indicates this by drawing an X on the paper. Person A closes his or her eyes. Person B starts about 20 feet away and slowly walks toward Person A. Person A repeats the word, "OK" when he/she feels Person B in his/her personal space and it feels comfortable. When this begins, Person B writes "OK" on the piece of paper and continues walking. Person A says, "STOP" when Person B gets too close to feel comfortable. When this happens, Person B writes "STOP" on the paper. Person A opens eyes and looks down to see if his/her predictions were correct.

**138**                                              **Peace Tool # 59**

## *Continuation* KNOW YOUR PERSONAL SPACE

### Questions for Discussion:

1.  What did you notice about your ability to sense other people in your personal space?

2.  Were you surprised by anything you learned about yourself? Why or why not?

3.  When you were Person A, what were some of the feelings you had when Person B was moving toward you?

4.  As Person B, did you sense when Person A became uncomfortable with your presence? Why or why not?

5.  When someone "invades your space" do you feel OK about telling him or her to back off? Why or why not?

6.  Have you ever thought about your person space as "Your right?" What does this mean to you?

### When you have a quiet moment by yourself, try this activity...

Close your eyes and take a few deep breaths. Feel your body relax. Feel your lungs expand and as they do, say to yourself, "I have a right to be here." Feel the space you take up on earth. Keep breathing deeply and slowly and let yourself know that you belong here. You have every right to take up the space you do. Tell yourself you are special, important, and that the space you take up is special and important, too.

Take as long as you want, but try to do this for at least five minutes. When you open your eyes, be aware of how you feel inside and how you feel about yourself. Do this activity a few times and you will notice that when you are with others, you will find yourself protecting your personal space more effectively!

**Peace Tool # 60**

# PEACE SMARTS IN CROWDED PLACES

**Directions: Part I:** On the rungs of the ladder below are ways people often feel crowded.

＊     In the space below each rung, write how <u>you</u> would feel (or have felt) in that situation.

＊     Then go on to Part II.

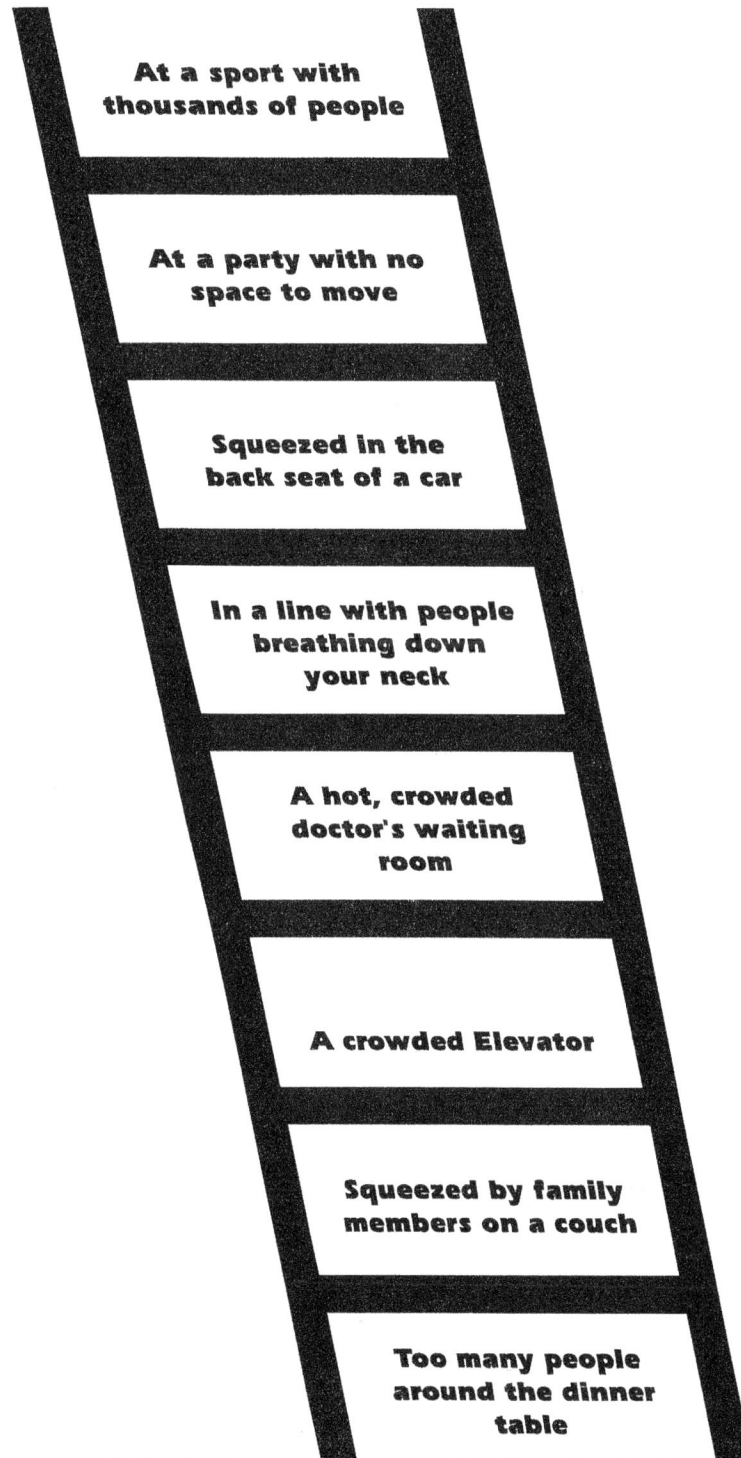

At a sport with thousands of people

At a party with no space to move

Squeezed in the back seat of a car

In a line with people breathing down your neck

A hot, crowded doctor's waiting room

A crowded Elevator

Squeezed by family members on a couch

Too many people around the dinner table

## Peace Tool # 60

## *Continuation* PEACE SMARTS IN CROWDED PLACES

**Directions: Part II:** Discuss your feeling in the situations above with a partner or in a small group. Then read the techniques below. Which ones would you like to try? Which ones do you think would work best for you?

# Feeling Crowded?—Some Things You Can Do

**1** **If you are actually being squeezed by person/s next to you...**
politely ask them if they could move over a little. If they can't take a few deep breaths and try thinking about something else for awhile. Make the time pass faster by concentrating on a goal or dream of yours—the more often you picture this in your head, the more likely it will come true for you. Work hard to stay inside your head with anything that will distract you from the physical discomfort. If you feel yourself getting angry, Stop and think, "How long before I can get out of this situation?" "Is there a way I can get out sooner?" If not, concentrate hard on breathing and relaxing. The time may pass quicker than you think!

**2** **When in a crowded elevator or at a crowded dance or party...**
pull yourself inside of yourself! How? Become more aware of yourself than the people around you. Practice this at home by looking at yourself in the mirror. First, see yourself and all the other things in the mirror, too—whatever is in the background. Now slowly take your attention away from all those things by closing your eyes and going within for a few minutes. Now, open your eyes. Can you practice going within yourself with your eyes opened? Try it and see what happens. You will gradually find that you can still be aware of your external environment, but you won't be so bugged when you can stay focused on the quiet place within yourself.

**3** **Feeling yourself getting angry when waiting in a crowded doctor's office?**
One cure for this is to always have a book or magazine with you that you can read. Something you are really interested in so the crowds and the waiting won't get to you. You will be so immersed in your reading, you might not even hear your name when it's called!

**Peace Tool # 60**

# PEACE SMARTS IN CROWDED PLACES *Continuation*

**4 Assert yourself.**
For instance, if you are in a comprising position of any kind, speak up and let your preference be known if that is safe to do. If not, remove yourself from the situation. It's important to learn which situations are safe or comfortable for you and which aren't. Try to stay out of and be aware of dangerous situations.

**5 Practice being invisible.**
If you are in a crowded room or on a crowded street and would like to pass by unnoticed by others, try this visualization trick: Imagine that you are covered head to toe with a dark blanket or cloak. See yourself being fully covered, so that others cannot see you. Maintain this image in your mind as you walk through the crowds. Sounds strange? Try it before you judge it. You may just be surprised at how well it works!

**6 Know that your reactions are normal.**
It's natural to get upset when feeling crowded. As a matter of fact, research shows that when too many animals are in a small space, their stress level goes up. If you find yourself getting impatient or angry, take a moment to talk with yourself. The conversation inside your head may sound like this: "It's normal for me to feel impatient now. There are just too many people on the street right now. This is what I get for leaving my holiday shopping to the last minute. I know now that I just don't like crowds, so I will relax and try to enjoy it. But next year, believe me, things will be different!" Talk gently to yourself when you feel your self under stress. It can make a big difference!

# 142

## THE IMPORTANCE OF PERSONAL BOUNDARIES

**Directions:** How important are personal boundaries to you?

✳ After each statement, check whether the boundary is Very Important, Somewhat Important, or Not Important at all.

✳ Think carefully about each type of boundary listed before you indicate your response.

✳ When you are finished, share your responses with a few friends and/or trusted adults.

| Boundary | Very Important | Somewhat Important | Not Important |
|---|---|---|---|
| Stopping your boyfriend/girlfriend when you are feeling uncomfortable with any sexual advance. | | | |
| Checking who is at the door before you open it | | | |
| Telling friends you can't meet them when you just don't feel like it. | | | |
| Asking the person next to you in line to take a step away from you. | | | |
| Standing, instead of sitting and being squeezed, on a crowded bus. | | | |
| Having a bedroom to yourself or a space you can go to be alone. | | | |
| Telling people not to interrupt you when you have work to get done. | | | |
| Telling an adult you feel uncomfortable with his or actions or words toward you. | | | |
| Asking the kid behind you in class to stop banging on the desk. | | | |
| Keeping a secret for a friend. | | | |
| Refusing to gossip about people. | | | |
| Refusing help when you want to accomplish something by yourself. | | | |
| Making sure all your doors and windows are locked. | | | |
| Not talking to strangers. | | | |
| Not accepting a ride or gift from someone you don't know well. | | | |
| Refusing to give the class clown attention. | | | |
| Walking confidently with eyes straight ahead on a crowded city street. | | | |

**Peace Tool # 62**

# SAYING "NO" TO A FRIEND

## Directions: Think about the following:

Everyone wants respect. How we show respect to others and how we get respect in return are important in keeping our personal integrity. Sometimes kids think they can gain respect from others by force, domination, verbal abuse, or intimidation. They have learned something that has worked for them in the past with some other people. But pressuring friends leads to trouble, not respect.

Maintain your confidence and self-respect by not being afraid to say "No" when a friend is trying to get you do something you would rather not do. These situations are the ultimate test of our ability to keep personal boundaries. They can be challenging, but with practice **YOU CAN DO IT!**

## Practice being peace-smart by practicing being assertive.

* Below are several situations.

* With a partner choose a few to role play.

* Switch roles so you experience both sides.

**Helpful hint:** The person who is trying to stay out of trouble could do any of the following during the role play:

* Look your harassing friend straight in the eye and firmly tell him/her, "Thanks, but I would rather not."

* Make up an excuse that you are needed elsewhere and quickly leave.

* Keep repeating the same thing, like "I don't want to now." or "Let's just drop it." Repeat it until you are more nagging than your friend!

* Stay calm and remember that you don't have to do something you don't want to.

* Clearly make your own needs known. "Please leave now, I need to get my homework done." "I have to go, I'm late for a doctor's appointment."

## Role play situations:

Jeff, from your English class, wants you to steal the answers for an upcoming test because you sit close to the teacher's desk and can get to them easily.

Bonnie wants you to punch out her boyfriend for her because he cheated on her.

Magi just stole some clothes from the department store. She is trying to get you to take a few because they are in your size, too. You would rather not.

Your friend from another school wants you to sneak him into the school dance. You know he is carrying a gun and this could be very dangerous.

# ROAD RAGE AND YOU

**Directions:** Whether you are the driver or the passenger—it's bound to happen... Someone cuts off the car you are in; someone speeds past you recklessly; someone behind you honks and honks his horn because he is impatient with you.

With more cars on the freeways, come increasing levels of frustration. And with that, more people prone to violent behaviors. Learning how to be peace-smart on the road is now more important than ever.

## Below are familiar situations.

With a partner:

* Read each one.

* Then select and discuss the peace-smart option (or options) you would choose in each situation.

## Situations:

Your car is acting up and you need to pull over, off the freeway. It is 11PM in a remote part of town.

An irate driver passes you very quickly then slows down in front of you. You have to brake quickly. The driver continues to go very slowly, seemingly to get you mad.

You see a car pulled over with its hood up. It is pouring down rain and you would like to help the driver.

Your blood is boiling because the driver in front of you nearly hit you, he's honking and giving you the finger like it's your fault.

You are with good friends at a party. It's time to go home and your buddy who was the so-called designated driver is drunk. He insists on driving you home.

This is your first time driving alone in this part of the city and you have to admit, "You're lost." It's 2 AM. Now what?

This is not your imagination but a car is following you. You see it everywhere you are going and you can't lose it.

## Peace Smart Options:

As hard as it is, strive to remain calm when other drivers start getting to you. Use the stress reduction techniques that you know, such as deep breathing and calming self-talk. **Never** get out of your car and confront the driver. With so many people carrying weapons, this is just too dangerous to do.

## Peace Tool # 63

# ROAD RAGE AND YOU *Continuation*

Buy a large reflector which states: **Call Police**. At all times keep this in your glove compartment and put it in your front or rear window when stranded. Keep your doors locked and stay in your car until authorities arrive.

If at all possible carry a cellular phone in your car to use in emergencies.

Always ask a friend to accompany you when you are driving in unfamiliar areas.

When lost and it is late at night, find the nearest 24-hr. mini-mart and ask for directions there. Be courteous and friendly.

Drive with all the doors locked.

Do not give eye contact to drivers next to you when stopped at a red light. Keep your eyes straight ahead and resist any acknowledgment if someone shouts, calls you names, or tries to get your attention in any way.

Keep your car in good working order. Change oil regularly. Check tires, water level frequently. Do all you can to prevent a breakdown.

Keep a gallon of water in your trunk in case your car overheats.

If your car has broken down put your hazard lights on. If someone stops to help you, roll down the window slightly. Tell the person, "The police are on their way," (even if they aren't). Add, " I'd appreciate it if you may want to call them again, just to be sure they got the message." Roll up the window and signal to the person that you are OK and thanks for the help. Wait until the proper authorities arrive before you unlock your doors and get out of your car.

If you get a flat tire, drive carefully on it until you reach a safe, well-lit and well-traveled area.

Don't stop to assist a stranger whose car has broken down. Instead, help by driving to the nearest phone and calling police to help.

If you are being followed, don't drive home. Go to the nearest police or fire station and honk your horn. If that is not possible, drive to an open gas station or other business where you can safely call the police. Don't leave the car unless you are certain you can get inside the building safely. Try to obtain the license plate number and description of the car following you.

Do not drink and drive. Do not get in a car with a driver who has been drinking alcohol. Always have a designated driver, who does not drink at all, when out with friends. If no one agrees, then make sure you take on this responsibility. Remember, **not one drink** when you are driving!

# 146

## SHOPPING WISELY

**Directions:** Much of the crime at stores or in malls is limited to pickpocketing and theft. Tricks are played on shoppers to catch them unaware and unprepared.

### Below are some of these tricks.

* With a partner or in a small group, read and discuss them. Knowing these tricks is the first step to avoid being victimized by them.

* Then with your friend/s, under each trick write what you could do in that situation to avert a problem.

* Use the lines below each one to write down your ideas.

### Watch out for these tricks while you are shopping:

You are at the phone booth in a mall making a call. Your bag with your new shoes is at your feet. A person comes by and asks you directions. While you are focused on helping that person, someone else walks up from the other direction and takes your bag.

### To prevent this from happening, you could:

_____

_____

_____

_____

_____

## Peace Tool # 64

# SHOPPING WISELY *Continuation*

You're waiting in line to pay for another purchase. You have a few bags from other purchases you have made. They are at your feet as you are getting out your wallet. Someone walks by and points to several dollars lying on the floor. He or she asks, "Did you drop that money?" It's not your money, but it is too much of a temptation to say, "No." As you stoop down to pick it up, the person quietly walks away with the shopping bags you left unprotected.

**To prevent this from happening, you could:**

_____

_____

_____

_____

_____

You're in the mall restaurant, waiting in line to pay your bill. You have your purse and your shopping bag with you. Someone in back of you squirts ketchup on your upper shoulder. He or she then points out to you, "Look, you have something on your coat." You turn your head, see it, put your purse and bag down, in order to start cleaning it up. The "nice person" keeps your attention focused on this task. A second crook grabs your purse and bag and hurries away.

**To prevent this from happening, you could:**

_____

_____

_____

_____

_____

# 148

## STREET SMARTS

### Directions:

**First:** Read the following quote from philosopher, Eric Fromm. Then on the lines below it, write down what you think it means.

### "Warlikeness grows in proportion to civilization."

_____

_____

_____

**Second:** With a friend or in a small group, discuss the following questions:

* When groups are gathered together is there more a likelihood of violence? Why or why not?

* Does your town have a problem with youth loitering on the street? If, so what do you think should be done about it?

* If you see someone muscling someone or provoking a fight, do you feel comfortable reporting it? Why or why not?

* What makes you feel uncomfortable when you are walking down your city streets?

* What can you do about it?

**Third:** Read the following list of things to do while you are walking on the street to stay safe. Discuss them with others. Tell which ones you have already tried and how they worked for you. Tell which ones you would like to try and give reasons for your choices.

### Stay street smart by:

* Being alert to your surroundings and the people around you.
* Staying in well-lit areas.
* Walking confidently at a steady pace on the side of the street facing traffic.
* Walking close to the curb. By avoiding doorways, bushes, and alleys, you also avoid the chances of being assaulted.
* Wearing clothes and shoes that give your freedom of movement.
* Not walking alone at night and always avoid areas where there are few people.
* Being careful when people stop you for directions. Always reply from a distance, and never get too close to the car.
* Attracting help if you are in trouble with a scream, yell, or calling "Fire!"
* Walking to a well-populated are if you feel you are being followed.

**(Adapted from the booklet, "How can I reduce my risk of being assaulted?"**
**by the National Crime Prevention Council and the National Sheriff's Association.)**

              

# BECOME PEACE-SMART ABOUT MEDIA VIOLENCE

## Did you know...

### Directions: Think about the following statistics:

* MTV contains twice the amount of violence found in prime-time programming. Most of this violence is toward women.
* By age 12, kids will have seen more than 20,000 murders and 80,000 assaults on television.
* Experts believe that 50% of real-life murders, rapes, and assaults are directly related to media violence.

### What does this have to do with you?

* Below are the three different activities.
* Do all three over the next couple of weeks.
* Get to know the importance of becoming peace-smart about media violence!

### Activity 1:

Below are four common effects from watching too much violence on the screen. Discuss each with a parent or friend. Do you know someone who shows these characteristics? Do you know a young child who watches too much violence?

#### Four common effects from watching too much violence:

* Becoming more mean and aggressive
* Becoming more fearful; feeling hopeless and helpless; seeing the world as more dangerous than it really is
* Becoming desensitized to real-life violence; not being caring or compassionate
* Seeking more and more violence for entertainment—on screen and off

### Activity 2:

Keep track of violent acts while you watch TV. You could count the number of both physical and emotional acts of violence. How many did you come up with in a half hour TV program? A two hour movie? Your favorite video game? (See the next page for types of violent acts seen on the screen.)

**Peace Tool # 66**
*Continuation*

# BECOME PEACE-SMART ABOUT MEDIA VIOLENCE

## Examples of physical violence:

* hitting, punching
* pushing, shoving
* shooting, knifing
* destroying property

## Examples of emotional violence:

* put-downs
* name-calling
* making jokes out of someone's misfortune
* racial slurs or sexist comments

## Activity 3:

Not all media violence is the same. Below are characteristics of sensational portrayals of violence and sensitive portrayals. Give examples of each type from the TV programs and movies you saw recently.

## Sensational violence:

* lots of fast-action sequences with graphic depictions of violence
* the perpetuator of the violence seems to be having fun
* little or no consequences of the violence are shown
* special effects keep the viewer excited
* the perpetuator of the violence seems "cool" or glamorous

### Examples of Sensational Violence:

_____
_____
_____
_____
_____
_____
_____
_____

## Sensitive Violence:

* action is varied with sequences seeming more like real life
* when violence happens, consequences are shown which make the viewer feel compassion
* there are few incidents of violence, but they are memorable for the lessons they entail
* makes the viewer know that violence toward others is wrong
* makes the viewer think about and want to do something about "man's inhumanity to man"

### Examples of Sensitive Violence:

_____
_____
_____
_____
_____
_____

(Note: Statistics taken from *Screen Smarts: A Family Guide to Media Literacy* by Gloria DeGaetano and Kathleen Bander, Houghton Mifflin, 1996.)

# VIOLENT VIDEO GAMES: WHAT DO THEY TEACH?

**Directions:** Below you will find a list of what you can expect to learn from violent video games and what you can expect from non-violent, educational video or computer games.

* Read each list.

* Then discuss the questions below with a partner or in a small group.

**Violent Games Teach...**                  **Non-Violent Games Teach...**

to expect to solve problems quickly         that problem-solving requires patience

data is constantly given                    sometimes we have to research information

choices are limited                         choices are unlimited

to use trigger finger to solve problem      to use head to solve problem

not to use your own imagination             to use your own imagination

follow someone else's rules                 make up your own rules

use the same option, violence              use many options to solve problems

to take the easy way out                    to value the ability to overcome a challenge

**For Discussion:**

1.  What do you think you learn from playing violent video games?

2.  Are violent video games appropriate for someone your age? Why or why not?

3.  Are violent video games appropriate for younger children? Why or why not?

4.  After reviewing the lists above, do you want to make more of an effort to play non-violent games? Why or why not?

5.  Imagine an alien from outer space whose first contact with our society is a violent video game. What assumptions about our society will the alien make from playing a violent video game?

6.  Tell what you think of the following statements:

> "Street Fighter II made more money in video game arcades than
> Jurassic Park made in movie theaters—over a half-billion dollars."
> "On average, American children who have home video game machines
> play with them about one and a half hours per day."

# 152

## VIOLENT VIDEO GAMES: WHAT DO THEY TEACH?

**Make a Difference...**Want to see more meaningful, non-violent video games for kids your age? Write a letter! Express your concerns. Tell the video game manufacturers what peace-smart kids want! Write a letter and have your friends sign it, too. Remember there is power in numbers— youth make up 48% of the US population—and are the prime users of video games. The manufacturers will listen to you!

**Nintendo of America, Inc.**
Corporate Communications Manager
4820 150th Ave. NE
Redmond, WA 98052
(425) 882-2040
FAX: (425) 882-3585

**Sega of America**
Consumer Services 240 D
Shoreline Drive
Redwood City, CA 94065
(415) 508-2800
FAX: (415) 802-1338

**Philips Electronics**
Phillips CD1
Customer Service
100 East 42nd St.
New York, New York 10017
(212) 850-5000
FAX: (212) 850-5362

**3DO**
Customer Service
600 Galveston Drive
Redwood City, CA 94063
(415) 261-3454

Note: Statistics are taken from Alison Wells, ed.,
*Speak Up: A How-To Guide for Making a Positive Change in the Media,*
Mothers Against Violence in America, 1995, p. 24.

# NEWS: GLORIFYING CRIME?

**Directions:** Follow these steps. Learn peace-smart ways to watch the news.

**Step 6:** With your friend, write what you would do to change the reporting of violent crime.
How could you as a journalist or as a TV news producer, report these crimes more sensitively?
Use the lines below to explain what you would do.

**Step 1:** Watch the evening news and pick a news report of a violent crime.

**Step 5:** Repeat Steps 1-4 on a different day with a friend.

**Step 4:** Which report, TV or newspaper, gave you more objective information? Which seemed more hyped to you? Why do you think that was so?

**Step 2:** Now find that same report in your local paper.

**Step 3:** Read the report. What information is in the newspaper that was left out of the TV report. Anything?

_____

_____

_____

_____

_____

# 154

## *Continuation* NEWS: GLORIFYING CRIME?

### Other activities:

1. Role play a news report of violence the way you would like to see it happen. Discuss your reasons for making the changes that you do.

2. Write a newspaper article about a violent crime from the perspective of the victim of that crime. How does this perspective differ from a journalistic one?

3. Interview younger children who watch TV news on a regular basis. Find out if they are more fearful than children who don't watch TV news. Begin a campaign in your neighborhood for parents to monitor how much violence children see on TV news.

4. Tape and watch two different news programs aired on the same day. Then watch them again and compare the two: What are the similarities? The differences? Are the stories arranged differently? Does one report stress violent crime more than the other? Is more or less time devoted to the same news stories? Compare the anchors, the reporters, the sets, the graphics, the chitchat, the number of special reports, and the commentaries. Jot down some of your ideas and share them with friends or family. What are their observations?

**Peace Tool # 69**

# CHOOSING TO BE MEDIA LITERATE

**Directions:** Is it realistic for teens to stay away from media violence? Probably not. But teens do not have to become victims of media violence. That is, the violence they see on TV, in movies, or video games, does not have to affect them negatively.

Becoming "media literate" about media violence is one way to practice being peace-smart about the entertainment you choose.

### Below are ways to be media literate about media violence.
*   Check the column which applies to you.

*   Then discuss your responses with a friend.

*   Over time, with practice, what can you expect from your new way of viewing media violence?

| Media Literacy Skills | Already Do | Can Start Doing | Not Likely To Do |
|---|---|---|---|
| 1. Try to figure out non-violent ways to solving the problems presented. | | | |
| 2. Watch with a "thinking mind," not believing everything I see. | | | |
| 3. Ponder what watching this violence really is teaching me. | | | |
| 4. Work at understanding how screen violence makes me more compassionate to human suffering. | | | |
| 5. Know the importance of monitoring my intake of too much media violence. | | | |
| 6. Choose video games which test my mental skills more than my "trigger finger." | | | |
| 7. Discuss with friends how media violence can contribute to real-life violence. | | | |
| 8. While watching, predict how the script writer will resolve the conflict. | | | |
| 9. Think about how different portrayals of violence make me feel different emotions. | | | |
| 10. Watch myself carefully to see if I am imitating attitudes or behaviors I see on TV or in the movies. | | | |
| 11. Choose more entertainment which fits my life's goals and will help me stay peace-smart. | | | |
| 12. Steer younger children I know away from watching media violence. | | | |
| 13. Think about my responsibility to others in informing them about the effects of a steady diet of media violence. | | | |
| 14. Write letters to producers or ad agencies which continually show violence as an acceptable way of life. | | | |
| 15. Commit myself to watch less media violence. | | | |

# Peace Projects

## 1 Peace: Live it or rest in it.

MTV's harsh warning was a public service announcement the network ran to make kids think about the ultimate consequence of violence: death. Design a public service announcement (PSA) which will send a message about the importance of practicing peace smarts. The PSA could air on your local TV stations. Brainstorm what you think are the most important things teens should know about being peace-smart. Think about ways to explain that once a person understands the need for peace, he or she doesn't really want or need a violent lifestyle. A teacher or someone at your local cable station can help you put your ideas into a short video for a "service commercial." Join with other organizations to get your announcement to air in conjunction with things happening in your community related to stopping violence.

## 2 Practice being Peace-Smart through role play.

Get together with some friends and act out the various roles of a violent crime. (Don't really hurt each other!). Someone should play the victim, someone else, the perpetrator, and one or several others, the police who come into the situation and intervene.

**A 911 call takes place...**the officers arrive...

Is there a confrontation?

* What is said by each?

* What is the result?

* In stepping into one of these roles what did you learn about the victim, perpetrator, the officers?

* Change roles. What did you experience about the humanity of each person? Discuss with your friends what you learned and how it can help you practice being peace-smart in your daily routine.

# Peace Projects

**3** **Create a Volunteer Newsletter.**
We know that the more help and encouragement people receive, the less likely they are to be violent. Work with local businesses to create a volunteer newsletter.

The newsletter could lists skills offered by people in the community who want to volunteer their time and it could feature non-profit organizations who are seeking volunteers.

Here's what to do to get started:

**First:** approach individuals, both adults and youth, who want to offer volunteer services. Explain this project and enlist their help and support.

**Second:** approach non-profit organizations in your neighborhood that use volunteers and ask them if you put together a community newsletter, would they use it to let others know about what types of volunteers their organizations need, without any costs to them?

**Third:** approach local businesses and show them the list of non-profit organizations who would use such a service. Ask the business owners if they would like to advertise in the newsletter for a fee. Also, ask them if they would be willing to make copies of the newsletter available to their patrons at no cost.

**Fourth:** approach a printing company in your neighborhood. Show the manager the list of non-profit organizations and the list of businesses who want to participate in this project. Ask if he/she would be willing to donate computer and printing services in order to advertise in the newsletter.

**Fifth:** once you have gotten all the support you need, get the entries and the ads from everyone you talked with. Once printed, distribute your newsletter to the participating local businesses. Follow up on a regular basis to see if the non- profit organizations have gotten volunteers through your newsletter. Evaluate results and plan another newsletter for next year!

# Bullying Statistics

- 1 out of 4 teens are Bullied.
- 43% of kids have been bullied online.
- 9 out of 10 LGBT kids are harassed at school & online.
- Daily160, 000 students stay home, fearful of being bullied.
- 1 out of 5 kids admits to being a bully.
- 43% fear harassment in school bathroom.
- 282,000 First - Fifth graders are physically attacked monthly.
- 80% bully altercations ends up in a physical fight.
- 1/3 of students surveyed heard bully threats to kill someone.
- 2 out of 3 kids say they know how to make a bomb. And know where to get info'.
- Playground statistics - Every 7 minutes a child is bullied. Adult intervention - 4 %.  Peer intervention - 11%. No intervention - 85%. The average child has watched 8,000 televised murders and 100,000 acts of violence before finishing elementary school

US Secret Service Report: Bullying was a factor in 2/3 of the 37 school shootings.

**In schools where bullying programs are implemented- Bullying is reduced by 50%.**


# How to Avoid A Bully

If you know your sibling, a neighbour, or friend is being bullied and the problem hasn't been resolved in school or with help from the bully's parents – don't advise them to retaliate or fight back. Bullying doesn't stop by fighting or bullying back. It can quickly escalate into violence, and someone getting injured. Instead, it's best to walk away from the situation, hang out with others, tell an adult. If the bully is physically abusive, hits, or destroys property police intervention may be necessary.

1.      **Use the buddy-up system**. Use a different bathroom if a bully is nearby and don't go to your locker. Buddy up with a friend on the bus, in the hallways, or at recess — wherever the bully is. Offer to do the same for a friend.

2.      **Hold the anger.** Bullies thrive on upsetting you and watching you squirm. It makes them feel powerful. Use 'cool-down' techniques to keep off of a bully's radar. Counting to 10, deep

breathing or walking away. Learn to a wear a "poker face" until you clear of any danger, smiling or laughing provokes bullies.

**3.** **Act brave, walk away, and ignore the bully.** Firmly and clearly tell the bully to stop, then walk away. Practice ways to ignore the hurtful remarks, like acting uninterested or texting someone on your cell phone. By ignoring the bully, you're showing that you don't care. Eventually, the bully will probably get bored with trying to bother you.

**4.** **Tell an adult.** Teachers, principals, parents, and lunchroom personnel at school can all help stop bullying. It's their responsibility to keep all students safe.

**5.** **Talk about it.** Talk to someone you trust, such as a guidance counselor, teacher, sibling, or friend. They may offer some helpful suggestions, and even if they can't fix the situation, it may help you feel a little less alone.

**Remove the incentives.** If the bully is demanding your lunch money, start bringing your lunch. If he's trying to get your music player, don't bring it to school.

# Cyber-Bullying

Cyber attacks beat down the human spirit with a 24/7 reminder that you are hated, abused, and powerless. Whether the attack is on a social networking site like Facebook, chat rooms, phone calls or text messages...the result is the same - sadistic. Malicious rumors are spread that can lead to exclusion of the victim. And so it was with Jeffrey Johnston, a kind young man who showed great promise to those that knew him. Tired of being called "fat", "faggot" by perpetual cyber assaults. So fragile, questioning his sexuality, worthiness... he couldn't take it anymore. He couldn't see a future, how to fit in the world, or that it would get any better. Broken spirited... Jeffery took his life, he was only fifteen.

Outraged, Debbie Johnston, Jeffery's mother advocated that it would never happen to another child. After a relentless effort, in honor of her son, **The Jeffrey Johnston Act** passed in Florida. School Districts must ban harassment, intimidating, cyber-bullying, and report all incidences', investigate allegations, outline consequences for students and teachers who violate policy and bullies must be referred to counseling and proper authorities. Victims ' families must be notified what has been done to protect their children.

# NATIONAL RESOURCES

## National Domestic Violence Hotline

### 800 – 953-2207

Hotline provides information, support, and referral to battered women's shelters in your area.

## Boys & Girls Club Of America – (562) 490-6174

Offers after-school programs for youth. Anti-violence programs for at-risk, foster care, and local neighborhood kids. Services to promote health, social, educational, vocational, and character development. Drug and alcohol prevention, delinquency intervention, and leadership development.

## Teen/Youth Suicide Hotline - 866 210.3388
## Big Brothers and Sisters of America –
## 800 207-7567

Mentoring Program- Above number will put you in touch with Local program.

## Alanon Teen/Family Groups. (800) 344-2666

Helping families affected by alcohol and addiction. There are special groups for children and teens.

## Join "Peace Smarts – Bully Project" 4 Teens & Youth Voices/Action
## www.peacesmarts.com

MerrieWay Community, a non-profit 501C3, is producing Byron Fox's short film, " Bully Proof Vest" to support "Peace Smarts" curriculum. It's a riveting expose of a teen bullied into the trappings of a youth gang... and the devastating consequences that befall him... and his family.

After meeting with Bill and Hillary Clinton, Byron Fox, who served as our national youth spokesperson, shared these moving comments.

"In the East Room at the White House I met the President of the United States. When
I shook President Clinton's hand... I didn't gaze into his eyes... I looked at his hand. This was the hand that shook Martin Luther king's hand that shook President Kennedy's hand. Now, when I look at my own hand, I realize it is a part of history. Greeting each other with respect, and shaking hands is a true honor."
**Byron Fox**

☮☮☮

It's our privilege to share Peace Smarts, a legacy, entrusted to you. Together we've planted seeds for you to nurture in Peace and Harmony.

Your truth, your voice, your right actions will inspire change in the world. Collaborate; spread the word, a vision of equality will prevail.  YES Peace Maker ...
BE REAL, LAUGH & LOVE.

# Teens & Youth Listen Up...

"Peace Smarts" Opportunity for YOU.

☮ Youth anchors cover local events - and you can create your own video, on any issue of interest. Enter Peace Smarts Online Film Festival.

☮ Collaborative with friends and classmates - Share comments and photos. www.peacesmarts.com

**SHARE YOUR STORY – Be featured in Morph America book and video.**

A personal view... of growing strong, showing courage, spreading kindness. How you morphed violence into Peace, gave back to the community, counteracted bullying. How you express yourself creatively, and help other kids do the same.

**Share your story ... YOU are Special.**

**TEENS Bring Peace Smarts program to your school go to: www.peacesmarts.com**

**Gift a copy of "Peace Smarts" curriculum** - share it with your local school. 144 pg. reproducible techniques - benefitting over 2 million teachers, students, parents nationwide. No more excuses. Stop Bullying! Enough is Enough!

**YES! WE CAN DO IT!**

# PEACE SMARTS

## Certificate of Participation

_____

has successfully completed

**A National Peace Smarts Project**

*Merrie Lynn Ross*  _____
**Merrie Lynn Ross**  Date
**MWC, President**

**Merrie Way CommUnity**

# ADDITIONAL RESOURCES AVAILABLE

## www.peacesmarts.com

## BOOKS BY MERRIE LYNN ROSS

Bounce Off The Walls- Land On Your Feet

Life As An Improv' - HAHA Healers Series

Happy Heart Journal

Adventures of Funny Mummy

Peace Smarts Curriculum

Morph America Curriculum

Morph America 2 - Community

Nartikki – Soul Dancer

## Courses/Workshops/DVD's

The Bully Solution- Peace Smarts - DVD, course materials.

Peace Smarts Within E-Course with MP3's /mini book

HAHA Healers Teleseminar, E-Course, Live Workshops

Life As An Improv'-E-course, MP3's + Bonus Teleseminar.

Merrie Lynn is available for media interviews, live events, lecture and motivational speaker engagements, Tele-seminars, and workshops.

# ABOUT THE AUTHORS

**Merrie Lynn Ross** – multi award winning filmmaker/author/actor has starred in 35+ TV/films. Best known as daytime's first comedienne, she giggled into millions of viewer's hearts on 'General Hospital'. Internationally acclaimed as a child advocate, honored by President Clinton, she created "Morph America" and "Peace Smarts" curriculums, helping over two million families to create a culture of peace.

**Gloria DeGaetano, M. Ed** – **is** an educator with over 35 years experience – as a curriculum specialist, classroom teacher, University instructor, and public schools administrator. Currently as a teacher's trainer she consults with school districts nationwide. Ms. DeGaetano has written several books including Media Smarts 4 Young Folks and Screen Smarts: A Family Guide to Media Literacy.

# Enjoy this FREE Gift!

BYRON`S SERIES

## BE REAL, LAUGH & LOVE

BE Real, Laugh & Love's Inspirational content
will be sent to you with instructions. An amazing way into
your heart's desire and how to actualize your truth.

Go to ~ www.bereallaughlove.com

MediaMorphUs - publisher
www.merrieway.com

# PEACE NOTES

www.ingramcontent.com/pod-product-compliance
Lightning Source LLC
Chambersburg PA
CBHW062044090426

42740CB00016B/3009